UNDERDOG
RISE ABOVE WHEN YOU FEEL BELOW

Nick Graham

UNDERDOG
Rise Above When You Feel Below
Copyright © 2023 by Nick Graham

Published by Lucid Books in Houston, TX
www.LucidBooks.com

All rights reserved. No part of this publication may be reproduced, stored in a retrieval system, or transmitted in any form by any means, electronic, mechanical, photocopy, recording, or otherwise, without the prior permission of the publisher, except as provided for by USA copyright law.

ISBN: 978-1-63296-802-9
eISBN: 978-1-63296-635-3

Special Sales: Most Lucid Books titles are available in special quantity discounts. Custom imprinting or excerpting can also be done to fit special needs. Contact Lucid Books at Info@LucidBooks.com

"My entire career lacking the size in a sport that is geared toward taller players and feeling like the odds are stacked against me I would say has put me in the category of considering myself an underdog. This book is a resource for those who in some point in their careers will feel this sense that the odds are not in their favor.

I enjoyed this book because, as a competitor, it provides great insight and encouragement through experience and examples. Nick is a great person and his competitive experiences have allowed him to bring this book and concept to life. With the influence that he has had on the professional, and collegiate level of helping players get to their best, his expertise is a resource that encourages all who are able to be around him as well as all who will read his book."

MARKUS HOWARD
Former Denver Nugget guard (NBA) and current Professional Basketball player

"Aside from Nick's ability to train on the court, which I first experienced when I was in college, it's his ability to support and prepare those he works with mentally for what lies ahead that's most needed and impressive. I have been an underdog my entire career, and what's allowed me to overcome all of my competitive obstacles and live out my lifelong dream of becoming an NBA player is my mentality. This book will challenge, inspire, and transform all who read it and aid them in developing the mentality needed for them to reach their competitive goals."

MONTE MORRIS
Professional Basketball Player: Detroit Pistons (NBA)

"*Underdog* is a brilliant compilation of anecdotes and strategies aimed at helping underdogs around the world push their limits and achieve greatness. Having been in that position, I know this wisdom is universal and timeless. Nick's writing is both accessible and impactful. Part parable, part playbook, *Underdog* is a must-read for anyone seeking to gain a mental edge."

YOUSSEF ZALAL
UFC Fighter

"I met Nick During my time with the Denver Nuggets. What impresses me most about Nick a is not his on-court coaching but the impact he's had on athletes outside the lines."

MELVIN HUNT
NBA Basketball Coach

"When I was a college athlete, I was going through one of the toughest times of my life, dealing with underling mental health problems and feeling defeated. Then I met Nick. He was placed in my life just when I needed it the most. We started off with just basketball workouts, but then it became bigger than basketball. He became my perspective coach which strengthened my mentality, which led to my game elevating."

NIA WASHINGTON
Former Collegiate Athlete

"Nick is not just a friend; he is also an extremely positive influence on my life. He has mentored countless who have gone on to be successful not only in athletics, but also in other fields and professions. He is passionate, hardworking, and practices what he preaches. He has helped me make leaps and bounds in my career by assisting me into developing into a better player and person."

JIMMER FREDETTE
Professional Basketball Player

"Nick was huge in developing who I am today, both on and off the basketball court. From the time I was a youngster, he challenged me to strive toward excellence in whatever I was doing. He also influenced me never to compromise my character. I can confidently say I wouldn't be a professional basketball player today it it weren't for Nick's guidance."

SAM MASTEN
Professional Basketball Player

"When I met Nick I was coming off the hardest season I've ever had. I was broken mentally and physically. Nick instantly became more than just an exceptional trainer to me. He became a genuine friend. Nick encouraged me mentally and elevated my game. Our work together led to my return to the NBA and leading my team to a championship while playing overseas."

JULYAN STONE
Former NBA and Current Professional Player

"Nick is one of a kind. His ability to reach people, challenge people, and motivate others while also showing the ability to lead and show compassion is what makes Nick special."

TREY MOSES
Professional Basketball Player

Dedicated to the life and legacy of my day 1 underdog "Mikey,"
***SGT Michael Anthony Hagan-Daniel.*008*

I pray your underdog spirit lives on and is felt through this book.

To his mother and father, Carlos and Melanie, thank you for raising a real one. To his wife Quincy, he loved you dearly, and to the apple of his eye, Malachi, Mikey was so proud to be your father.

Michael Anthony Hagan-Daniel
May 11, 1994 - June 19, 2022

TABLE OF CONTENTS

FOREWORD: DIMITRIUS UNDERWOOD — 1

INTRODUCTION: WELCOME, UNDERDOG — 5

PREFACE: UNDERDOG LEMONADE — 9

1. UNDERDOGS STEP EVEN IF THEY CAN'T STEP BIG — 13
Hope | Encouragement | Support | Mentality

2. TYRESE MAXEY: YOU HAVE WHAT IT TAKES, BUT WILL YOU GIVE IT? — 17
Challenge | Passion | Support | Preparation | Excellence

3. KEEP YOUR MENTAL TANK FULL — 23
Mental Health | Perspective | Preparation | Endurance | Empowerment

4. IT AIN'T OK TO JUST BE OK! — 27
Excellence | Accountability | Mentality

5. ESTABLISH AND PROTECT YOUR STANDARD OF EXCELLENCE – 1ST HALF — 31
Challenge | Understanding | Preparation | Accountability

6. ESTABLISH AND PROTECT YOUR STANDARD OF EXCELLENCE – 2ND HALF — 37
Support | Hope | Endurance | Accountability | Nourishment | Understanding

7. ERIC GARCIA: BEING THE PARTY > ATTENDING THE PARTY — 43
Prioritization | Perspective | Hope

8. CHECKMATE — 49
Support | Hope | Affirmation | Empowerment

9. SKIP THE SKIPS — 55
Support | Affirmation | Hope | Mental Health | Blocking out the Noise

10. SWEET FRUITS NEED DEEP ROOTS – 1ST HALF — 61
Preparation | Perspective | Endurance | Support | Challenge | Mental Health

11. SWEET FRUITS NEED DEEP ROOTS – 2ND HALF — 67
Preparation | Empowerment | Support

12. THEY AREN'T PREPARING ON THE SAME LEVEL – 1ST HALF — 73
Support | Understanding | Perspective

13. THEY AREN'T PREPARING ON THE SAME LEVEL – 2ND HALF — 77
Endurance | Resilience | Encouragement | Empowerment | Affirmation
Nourishment

14. GEORGE CONDITT IV: PROGRESS PRECEDES PROMOTION — 81
Acceptance | Empowerment | Encouragement | Mental Health | Resilience | Hope

15. GEORGE CONDITT IV: RECIPE FOR OVERCOMING DEPRESSION — 87
Acceptance | Empowerment | Encouragement | Mental Health | Support | Hope

16. AGGRESSIVELY PURSUE EXCELLENCE, NOT PERFECTION — 95
Perspective | Encouragement | Support | Empowerment | Hope

17. KNOCK KNOCK: OPPORTUNITY – 1ST HALF — 101
Preparation | Nourishment | Resilience | Excellence

18. KNOCK KNOCK: OPPORTUNITY – 2ND HALF — 107
Preparation | Perspective | Empowerment | Mentality | Challenge

19. UNDERDOGS, ACTIVATE — 111
Preparation | Perspective | Endurance | Passion

20. DAYLEN KOUNTZ: TOUGH TIMES DON'T BREAK, THEY CREATE — 115
Support | Encouragement | Hope | Nourishment | Resilience

21. DESTINATION-DRIVEN, NOT TRANSPORTATION-FOCUSED — 121
Perspective | Prioritization

22. THEY CAN'T JUDGE WHAT THEY CAN'T SEE — 127
Affirmation | Support | Blocking Out the Noise

23. BRITTANY GRAHAM: SOMETIMES IMPATIENCE IS LEGITIMIZED — 131
Encouragement | Hope | Nourishment | Reparation | Understanding Mental Health

24. ENDURE THE NOS — 1ST HALF — 137
Understanding | Support | Resilience

25. ENDURE THE NOS — 2ND HALF — 143
Encouragement | Revivement | Nourishment | Perspective | Endurance Preparation

26. BRYCE COOK: LIVE IN LION — 151
Hope | Affirmation | Encouragement | Nourishment | Revivement Inspiration

27. GET WINS OR DIE TRYIN': HOW TO ENDURE NOS — 157
Preparation | Support | Encourement | Nourishment | Challenge

28. KARL PAYMAH: UNDERDOGS DON'T RUN AWAY FROM WALLS — 161
Preparation | Challenge | Support | Spirit of Excellence | Perspective

29. CARE HOW YOU COPE — 1ST HALF — 167
Mental Health | Perspective | Reparation | Preparation | Prioritization

30. CARE HOW YOU COPE — 2ND HALF — 171
Mental Health | Perspective | Support | Reparation | Preparation Prioritization Understanding | Empowerment

31. MEET THE UNDERDOGS — 179
Challenge | Perspective | Mentality | Spirit of Excellence

ACKNOWLEDGMENTS — 187

> If you're not living ambitiously enough to **BE AN UNDERDOG,** are you really living?
> —Nick Graham

FOREWORD
DIMITRIUS UNDERWOOD

Growing up, I had the same plan for my life as millions of boys my age: work hard and make the league (NBA). While that was the goal, like most young kids, what I didn't know was the odds of that happening were .01 percent. After high school, my hard work toward my goal of the NBA landed me a scholarship at the University of Texas at Dallas, a NCAA Division 3 school. This was a slight detour of the plan I had in mind, as most that make it to the NBA play their college ball at a Division 1 school. Even though I was at a D3, I didn't lose heart, and because of my dedication, I continually developed, and by the end of my sophomore year, I was arguably the best player in the conference. I dominated my next two seasons, was a two-time All-American, and racked up more awards than I could count.

By the end of my final season, I was a shark swimming in the kiddy pool. My success at that level fueled my dreams of becoming a pro even more. While that was the case, something was looming over me: doubt! While I was dominant at the D3 level, deep down, I wondered if I was truly as good as I thought and had what it took to become a pro ball player. While I doubted, I knew the only way I'd have a chance to reach my goal was to leave the pond full of fish and swim in the ocean amongst other sharks. This is why when they granted student-athletes an additional "covid year" because of the COVID pandemic, with my last year of eligibility, I knew D1 had to be my next move.

This move was how I became friends with Nick, a basketball trainer and life coach for athletes in Dallas. He was asked to help me prepare for the summer before the jump I was about to make from D3 to D1. My first encounters with Nick were unorthodox, to say the least. I had worked with plenty of skilled trainers before and expected this time to be no different. I expected Nick to help me polish my skills and get me physically ready for the next level, like all trainers do, but Nick had a different agenda.

While Nick cared about my physical development as a player, like all the others, he was much more concerned about my mental and emotional development as both a competitor and a person. Nick knew I could have all the skills in the world, but I would struggle to find and sustain success if I weren't mentally and emotionally prepared. I worked out with a small group of college players who identified as an underdog like me. At first, I doubted Nick's competence and questioned all his antics. Frankly, I thought he was giving me a load of BS. Early on in our training, he would criticize my work ethic and tell me things like, "You are not good enough to take reps off." I brushed off most of the things he said, but he seemed determined to pick a fight with me.

I would make minimal to no change in my approach, and with good reason, or, at least, I thought at the time, because of all the awards I racked up while playing D3, I had convinced myself that my way was good enough. I quickly learned that brushing off what a coach said worked with others, but it wouldn't fly with Nick. When Nick recognized there was no change in my approach, things hit the fan! He straight up told me, "I promise you I'm the most stubborn person in the gym." He followed that up by saying that while I was talented, he didn't want to continue to train me because I refused to work at the level he demanded of me.

I honestly thought he was crazy! He was getting paid to work me out, and I didn't need someone who was getting paid to train me "disrespecting" me. After all, "I'm a 2x All-American," I thought to myself! "What could he possibly teach me that I didn't already know?" Somehow, we made it through the altercations and constant head-butting, and as time went on, I noticed something different

FOREWORD

about Nick. While he demanded a lot out of me in workouts, he also invited us to breakfast and lunch (Nick is a foodie; I think he may secretly love the post-workout meals more than the training!) at least a few times weekly to pour into, support, hear us all, and if you know Nick, of course, crack jokes for some reason, Nick thinks he's a comedian! Although I couldn't see it then, time revealed Nick's true intentions, what felt like pointless criticism and conflict from Nick turned out to be calculated construction. Now that I am on the other side of it, as I reflect, I recognize that Nick empowered me to build the mental toughness while providing the emotional support needed to thrive at the D1 and now professional level.

Through every stage of my career, I'd always been overlooked and undervalued; even in my successes, people have found ways to discount my talents and abilities. While I used to fight that, Nick taught me to embrace it. My story proves what this book will lead you to discover, which is, that once you embrace the spirit of being an underdog, nothing will stop you. While it's true you will be overlooked, counted out, picked last, or whatever your specific obstacle may be, you will have what it takes to overcome it! Still, while that's the case, you'll discover, and thankfully, without Nick having to prove he's the most stubborn person in the gym, that you're not good enough to not give all you have and still reach your desired destination!

While I am not yet in the NBA, I overcame my doubt and am living my dream of making a living as a professional basketball player, which is why I am forever grateful that Nick is always the most stubborn person in the gym! I mentioned that we were all underdogs in our workouts, and because of our experience with Nick, we were equipped to overcome no matter what. We called ourselves the underdog gang. While you may not be in the same gym, you are reading and subscribing to the same book, which means you, too, are now a part of our gang! So, on behalf of Justin, CJ, Keyuan, Brandon, and Jase (the gang from the workouts), welcome!

Dimitrius Underwood

INTRODUCTION
WELCOME, UNDERDOG

Fellow Underdog:

Many go to, but few go through! If you really are 'bout this underdog life, please take heed to what Winston Churchill once said. "If you are going through hell, keep going!" One thing that's certain is your underdog quest will require you to experience hellacious encounters. While it's a guarantee you will run into them, what determines if your treacherous experiences are a dead-end destination of doom or a long-lasting yet endurable layover you'll eventually overcome? It's your underdog DNA—or lack thereof.

I'm sure you've heard this proverbial saying: "When life gives you lemons, make lemonade." That's the standard for underdogs everywhere, right? We should look at the nos, the closed doors, the pain, the haters, and all other hellish experiences as nothing more than life's lemons.

One of my favorite encouragers, Rick Warren, author of *The Purpose Driven Life*, frequently speaks of "redemptive pain." He explains that it's redemptive when your pain is used to help others. It's the best use of it, Warren says. One of the most uplifting concepts about our culture today is paying it forward. Colleen Murphy, author of *Murphys Don't Quit*, explains paying it forward as "a response to a person's kindness towards you." Author Rob Wolley further expands on the principle of paying it forward, declaring it's "the opposite of payback. It is repaying someone's act of kindness to you by an act of kindness to someone else."

I mention the concepts of redemptive pain and paying it forward to provide you with a perspective pivot as it relates to your life's lemons. The perspective pivot is often that the hell you go through ain't about you! And while it's quite painful, it's not punishment. It's purposeful. The purpose is for you to be kind enough to take the lemons life has given you and courageously pay it forward by turning life's nasty lemons into lemonade. You'll discover as you read this book what Walt Disney, Sylvester Stallone, the creator of the Original Recipe at KFC, and so many others did to provide inspiration and navigation for all of us who are on our journey through underdog hell.

There'd be no lemonade without lemons that go through the painful pressing process. And if you don't courageously go through your underdog hell—your pressing process—the lemons life gives you will be wasted. That is why we have to keep going, as Churchill said, because when our underdog spirit leads us through underdog hell, there's someone in our sphere of influence whose underdog soul thirsts and needs to be quenched with a sweet-tasting cup of underdog lemonade that can only be produced from the lemons of your life.

That's what makes us underdogs different and why we lean on Mandela's power quote about enduring difficulties: "Difficulties break some men but make others." We know that everyone who lives will be given lemons; however, most ain't 'bout this underdog life and will refuse to go through it without turning the nasty and bitter lemons of life into an example that will inspire others.

For example, had it not been for my underdog hero Bryce Cook who paid it forward by not quitting when times got tough, I would have never overcome difficulties and weathered the nos I needed to write this book. Writing this book is not paying Bryce back but paying it forward to you so you can beat your odds. And after you defeat those odds, there is no need to pay me back. Instead, kindly pay it forward for the underdog in your camp that's next up, which will redeem your pain.

INTRODUCTION

OVERTIME

If life has given you a lot of lemons, that just means you have the opportunity to make a lot of lemonade! This book is my lemonade to you and many underdogs worldwide. While enduring my underdog hell, I reminded myself that the more lemonade I wanted to serve others, the more lemons of life I had to bear. I wrote a whole book for underdogs, so clearly there were a lot of lemons to be painfully pressed! But often the hell you go through ain't 'bout you!

Cheers, and enjoy your lemonade!
Lemonade Nick

PREFACE
UNDERDOG LEMONADE

T.S. Eliot said, "If you aren't in over your head, how do you know how tall you are." That sums up what it means to be an underdog, to "darefully" compete at life in such a way that when your life is complete, you don't leave any life on the table. My hope for you after completing this book is that you're convinced to enthusiastically discover "how tall you are!"

When you commit to the underdog life, you must be emotionally and mentally supported, prepared, and strong because, for us underdogs, life is going to life, and it's going to life hard! While my background and experience are in competitive athletics, this book is not just for athletes but for any competitor who identifies as an underdog, be it an accomplished professional athlete like Tyrese Maxey. Or maybe an aspiring actor like my good friend Rodney, a future college athlete like my niece Ta'Lor, former athletes that lost their way and became obese only to transform into workout warriors and lose over 300 pounds combined like sisters, Reana and Alex Kaminski, or an aspiring gourmet chef, who works two jobs while he works his way up the culinary ladder like my favorite barista, Leonard.

Before we advance, let's come to an agreement on what it means to be an underdog and an understanding of how an underdog will overcome. The Oxford Language defines an underdog as "a competitor thought to have little chance of winning a fight or contest." Combine that with a powerful quote that we will frequently reference throughout this book from Nelson Mandela: "Difficulties break some men but make others. No axe is sharp enough to cut the soul of a sinner who keeps on trying, one armed with the hope that he will rise even in the end." That said, what qualifies the above-mentioned individuals to be underdogs is a collaboration of their competitive spirit and their ability to endure and overcome long-lasting adversity, which holds true for you.

By definition, if you aren't a committed and consistent competitor, you aren't an underdog, and this book won't serve you. On the other hand, if you are in need of nourishment to feed your competitive soul in order not to break when you experience difficulties, this book will satisfy your appetite and serve as "underdog lemonade" to quench your thirst.

Along with reading individually and chronologically, other ways to read include:

Emotion and Mental Specific
As mentioned, for an underdog, life will be hard, and there will be moments when an underdog needs inspiration specific to their situation or disposition. When those moments hit, and you require nourishment specific to your mental or emotional state as a competitor, the contents listed with each chapter are how that chapter will support you.

Team Development, Bonding, and Discussion
If you are an athletic, family, or corporate team, as a group, you can carve out time to read and discuss before or after practices, on game day, in weekly meetings, or in corporate team building.

Pre-Season Preparation
Consider Underdog your mental and emotional weight room! As an athlete, our strength coaches would prepare pre-season workouts to develop our muscles to withstand the stress of the upcoming season. Underdog will serve as your pre-season emotional and mental muscle development.

PREFACE

Off-Season repair and restoration
On the playing field, after the season, athletes must allow their bodies to be repaired and restored to ensure they are ready for upcoming seasons. Mentally and emotionally, we must do the same after treacherous, competitive seasons.

Perspective Pivot
As competitors, if we can't change it, we must change how we feel about it. Throughout the book, you will be coached to pivot your perspective.

Overtime
On the physical court, to thrive, athletes must be prepared to go overtime and "dig deeper." Here on the mental playing field, we will do the same. Overtime is concluding commentary to nudge you to get below the surface.

Lemon Drop
After each chapter, inspirational quotes will be provided for you to carry with you back to your competitive battlefields.

1. UNDERDOGS STEP EVEN IF THEY CAN'T STEP BIG

Hope | Encouragement | Support | Mentality

Current hip-hop culture identifies one who is smashingly successful in their pursuits as a "big steppa." Not so long ago on social media, there were posts on "how it's going versus how it started." The posts called for you to post a picture of you currently as a big steppa and a flick of you when you first began, when you were more of a crawler than a steppa.

Those "how it started vs. how it's going" posts revealed that most—if not all—steppas did not start off stepping big. Before stepping big, their steps were probably small yet consistent. Lao Tzu, author of *The Art of War*, once said, "The journey of a thousand miles begins with a single step."

Unfortunately, many underdogs never begin the journey from being overlooked, dismissed, and disrespected to overachieving and doing all that most assumed they couldn't do. The reason is that they are not prepared or equipped, and they don't believe they can be the big steppa they desire to be.

Underdogs, I have both bad news and good news for you. I'll start with the bad news. You are probably correct in assuming you are not equipped or prepared to be a steppa. Now for the good news. You don't need to be!

As you journey from where you are to where you desire to go, you will continually develop along the way. That's what Lao Tzu meant by "a single step." Unfortunately, most never begin the journey to being the steppa they are capable of because they get overwhelmed by incorrectly thinking they need to take a thousand big steps in one day. Deep down they know they are incapable of that.

Instead, as you pursue your best life, commit to taking at least one small step toward who you desire to be and what you want to achieve. As you do, you will eventually look back and try to see where you started. You will be so far along on your journey that you will realize you are closer to the finish line than you are to your starting point and that you might as well keep stepping!

OVERTIME

Identify your own "how it started vs. how it's going" moment. Doing so will remind you of the process of taking small steps daily to develop into a big steppa. To encourage you, I will share my process first.

After coaching basketball for a year at a small college, I realized I would have a greater impact as a trainer. I pivoted to training and even wrote weekly devotionals for college coaches and players. Unfortunately, when I first started, I wasn't a good writer. Maybe that's a bit harsh, but my writing was highly unpolished to the point that I cringe when I go back and read those devotionals.

I started those devotionals in 2008. That's my "how it started." My "how it's going" is my book of basketball-themed devotionals released in 2020—*God x Basketball: An Athlete's Playbook to Navigating Life with God's Word*. It has endorsements by some of basketball's biggest influencers. More importantly, I occasionally get messages from people I have never met telling me how my book has changed their life. That's right! "Big Steppa Nick" (lol). But when I started in 2008 with those hard-to-read devotionals, I was "Can't Even Step So I'm Just Going to Crawl Nick" (haha).

UNDERDOGS STEP EVEN IF THEY CANT STEP BIG

LEMON DROPS

"If you can't fly then run, if you can't run then walk, if you can't walk then crawl, but whatever you do you have to keep moving forward."

MARTIN LUTHER KING JR.

"Frequently stepping small in the right direction daily is better than infrequently stepping big in multiple directions."

NICK GRAHAM

"The world makes way for the man who knows where he is going."

RALPH WALDO EMERSON

"Courage doesn't always roar. Sometimes courage is the quiet voice at the end of the day that says I'll try again tomorrow.'"

MARY ANNE RADMACHER

2. TYRESE MAXEY: YOU HAVE WHAT IT TAKES, BUT WILL YOU GIVE IT?

Challenge | Passion | Support | Preparation | Excellence

Tyrese Maxey is one of the NBA's young rising stars. He's 22 years old, and once his rookie contract ends, his next contract will be valued at north of $200 million. I've been blessed to have had a front-row seat to Maxey's climb from a humble, hard-working high school hooper in Dallas to the multi-million-dollar NBA star that he is. During Tyrese's senior year in high school, I worked out with him at SandersFit, one of the nation's premier athletic performance centers, and rebounded for one of his trainers, Rod Clark, a few times with his on-court work.

Anyone who saw Tyrese as he pursued his lifelong dream of being an NBA star knows it was earned and not given. Tyrese didn't catch a break. Instead, he made his breaks and turned his dream into reality with the consistency with which he pursued greatness. His effort and focus always remained on 100. Not only did he never miss a workout, but he was always early and eager and stayed late to put in extra work. In addition to his Kobe Bryant-esque work ethic, Tyrese was extremely curious about excellence as he constantly sought out old heads and OGs to pick their brains on how he could level up and improve.

I subscribe to the notion that once great people reach greatness, they aspire to become even greater, which Tyrese did then and continues to do now. His growth mindset of excellence paved the way for him to dominate during his senior year at South Garland High School.

He reached most of his high school athletic goals—the most notable the McDonald's All-American Game for the top twenty-four players nationally. Even though Tyrese failed to reach his goal of winning a Texas high school state title, he still shone even in the loss. He set a record for most points scored—46—in the state tournament. After high school, Tyrese starred as a freshman for the University of Kentucky, which led him to declare for the NBA draft after just one season.

While Tyrese prepared for the NBA draft, another high school basketball player from the same area in Dallas also worked out at SandersFit. Let's call him Milt. Milt went to the same trainers and played for the same teams as Tyrese and many of the city's other top players did. Milt, a high school senior, was nowhere near the same player that Tyrese was, but after I watched him play a few games, I believed he had what it took to achieve his lifelong dream of earning a college scholarship.

As time passed, Milt and I continued to develop a friendship, and I started attending his games and practices. Milt had the potential to play at the next level, but when I watched him play, I saw that he showed flashes but lacked both the consistency and dominance needed to secure a college scholarship. He frequently expressed that his lack of on-court success and recognition from college coaches affected his confidence and often made him question if he even had what it took to play at the next level.

At season's end, Milt still had zero offers and was convinced that he was dealt a lousy hand athletically. He convinced himself that since he played for the same teams, worked out with the same trainers, and lifted at the same performance center as Tyrese and the other standout players, he'd been giving what it took just as they had. He believed that the reason he had no looks was because he just wasn't good enough.

While Milt's dreams were fading away, Tyrese's were just beginning. I had just watched an NBA pre-draft special. It was a behind-the-scenes day in the life of Tyrese's pre-draft preparation in California. Tyrese's first workout began at 5:30 a.m., and by 10:00 a.m., he had finished his third and last workout of the day. His trainer, Chris Johnson, explained that this was what they did daily. They did nothing special because the camera crew was following them around. As the special went on, Tyrese explained that he was simply giving what it took to get what he wanted.

That same day at 10:30 a.m., Milt hit me up with a phone call to develop a game plan so he could rally and make one more effort at earning a college scholarship. We made small talk before getting into a game plan, and I asked him how his day was going. His response was "slow motion" because he had late (school) start on Wednesdays, which meant he didn't have to be there until noon. Milt's slow-motion response inferred that he had not yet done anything productive.

After Milt's "slow motion" response, there was no need to go any further with any game planning. That response told me everything I needed to know. It told me why he was frustrated, and crying to me on the phone because his dream was dying. A few weeks later, Tyrese would be on the other side of the emotional spectrum and would be joyfully tearing up as NBA commissioner Adam Silver announced him as the 21st pick in the 2020 NBA draft. He realized that his lifelong dream had just come true. Milt's actions told me that by being in slow motion at 10:00 a.m. while Tyrese had already worked out three times by that time, Milt wasn't going to reach his goal, not because he didn't have what it takes but because he refused to give what it takes.

While it'd be easy to dismiss Milt sleeping in and Tyrese working out three times before 10:00 a.m. as a coincidence, it wasn't! It turned out that even though Milt and Tyrese worked out at the same place with the same people, their competitive habits were in stark contrast. While Tyrese held himself to a consistent standard of excellence and always aspired to be greater than he was the day before, Milt's habits were inconsistent and mediocre, and he was easily content with who he was as a player. While it's true that they both worked out at SandersFit and had the same trainers, Milt was always late, took pride in doing the bare minimum, and left as soon as the workout was over.

Rick Warren once said, "The person we lie to most often is ourselves." That was the case with Milt. He had convinced himself that he was getting slept on. Still, the truth was that Tyrese's habits allowed him to reach his dream and eventually become a $200 million man. Milt's refusal to give consistent excellence, which is what it took, was why he didn't get where he wanted to go. Before you turn the page and close the book on this chapter, learn from Milt, and do what he should have done earlier in his process. Ask yourself, and answer it honestly, am I giving what it takes to get what I want?

OVERTIME

I've found it true that most people don't make it, not because they don't have what it takes but because they won't give what it takes. I've also discovered another truth. The reason many won't give what it takes is that deep down they truly don't believe they have what it takes and are afraid to find out because if they give their all and fall short, they will feel like a failure. If that's you, I suggest you redefine what being a failure is and that *failing does not make you a failure.*

LEMON DROPS

"If you are willing to do more than you are paid to do, eventually you will be paid to do more than you do."

ANONYMOUS

"Goals you refuse to chase don't disappear — they become ghosts that haunt you."

JON ACUFF, FINISH

"Be strong in seasons where it feels like nothing, or it will always be what it is right now."

ANONYMOUS

3. KEEP YOUR MENTAL TANK FULL

Mental Health | Perspective | Preparation | Endurance Empowerment

One of my boys, Chef D, is a personal chef and nutritionist for NBA players. He explains that being a chef for athletes is much different than cooking for non-athletes. When he prepares for the general public, his sole focus is on pleasing his patrons' palates. When he cooks for his pros, the flavor of his food must be "bussin'," but it must also, as he calls it, "fuel their athletic performance."

He explained to me that what he prepares and how much he prepares is specific to the current needs of his athletes. For example, he told me that one of his hoopers, we'll call him Dre, was leading the team in minutes played late in the season, and they were fighting to stay in the playoffs. As you can imagine, everything the team needed from Dre was taking a toll on him. On top of that, the team was about to hit the road. On the road trip, they would play five games in nine days as they traveled in and out of five different cities.

Chef D knew that without the proper diet, Dre would be unable to endure the demands of carrying his team to the playoffs. He would be putting out way more than he was taking in. That is why Chef D planned to prepare a high volume of carbo-loaded meals. The caloric intake of the meals was far more than Dre was accustomed to, and Dre was full well before he finished the meals. When that occurred, Chef D implored him to finish his meal to ensure he had adequate intake. Because of Chef D's exquisite and strategic cuisine, Dre was able to endure the stress on the court and lead his team to the playoffs.

Most competitors agree that competition is 80 percent mental and just 20 percent physical. As we compete, many of us commit to doing the work to be physically prepared. However, we neglect our mental diet. So, underdog, as you continue on your journey, do like Dre and eat those carbs, but also feed your mentality. Make sure you are taking in more mental nourishment before your battles than you will be required to put out during them.

As you develop your mental diet with the intention of providing your competitive soul and spirit enough nourishment to push through the obstacles you will be required to overcome, take a note out of Chef D's playbook. Assess the rigorous schedule that awaits you and be prepared to load up—on carbs and on mental preparation and transformation. We need to be physically *and* mentally tougher than the tough times ahead.

Chef D says that food is the fuel that produces positive performance. And mental preparation, continued strengthening, and support are the fuels that produce and sustain our best possible performance. So here's to you keeping your mental tank full and never running out of gas!

OVERTIME

Competitively speaking, have you taken the time to establish a healthy mental diet? Is it one that provides you enough nourishment to be mentally prepared to push through?

If yes, make note of your regimen, and add two or three items that can strengthen you even more.

If no, list at least three things you can do to begin to be mentally prepared and mentally stronger. Then identify a mentor or teammate with an excellent mental preparation diet and ask them what their diet consists of.

LEMON DROPS

"If you can change your mind, you can change your life."

WILLIAM JAMES

"You must learn a new way to think before you can master a new way to be."

MARIANNE WILLIAMSON

4. IT AIN'T OK TO JUST BE OK!

Excellence | Accountability | Mentality

Underdog Dre, a high school senior who dreamed of earning a scholarship to play college basketball, had just finished playing in an AAU basketball tournament in front of college coaches.

After the game, I asked Dre how he thought he played, and he said, "I played alright." I was both concerned and shocked, not so much with what Dre said but how he said it. His disposition was one of not only contentment but satisfaction with his average performance.

Since Dre was in the spring of his senior year and still had no scholarship offers, it was not up for debate that he was in underdog territory. Unfortunately, while he was in an underdog circumstance, he clearly lacked the proper underdog mindset, which is why I was concerned.

Before I share my post-game conversation with Dre, I encourage you to embrace the underdog understanding that Dre had to first accept—you can't change the truth, but the truth can change you. The ball was in Dre's court to trust what I would tell him as fact and not cap. While the truths were harsh, I was convinced they'd change him for the better.

Once Dre was emotionally tough enough to receive the underdog truths and be changed for the better, I passionately yelled at him, "It ain't OK to just be OK." I made sure he understood he was an overlooked underdog with excellent dreams, not OK dreams. And because his goals were excellent and not just OK, there was no way he'd arrive at his desired destination of excellence if his performance was just OK. Dre digested what I said and rebutted with this: "I know I played OK, but I still had 16 points and 5 assists, which was solid. More importantly, I was still the best player on the floor, so why are you so tight?"

I had a rebuttal of my own. I first assured Dre he had the potential to reach his goals. I then explained that as an underdog, he had to understand and accept that our potential is not reached by comparing ourselves against others who are content with mediocrity but by establishing a personal standard of excellence and measuring our performance against that. John Johnson echoed that idea when he wrote, "Success bases our worth on a comparison with others. Excellence gauges our value by measuring us against our own potential." This is what Dre and every other underdog must realize and why they must not settle for short-term success but instead elevate toward excellence.

I continued talking with Dre, telling him that the standard of excellence we underdogs establish demands that an OK performance, even if we have good numbers and outperform the field, is never acceptable. Instead, as underdogs committed to excellence, dominance is the desired destination. And while we may sometimes fall short of dominance, the fact that we are committed to wholeheartedly striving for it in all we do provides us with the best chance to reach our underdog dreams of excellence.

Before Dre left, I sent him on his way with a few underdog declarations that he could use to establish his personal underdog standard of excellence. I hope you'll do the same.

Dominance is the desired destination. When I evaluate my performance, I'm not satisfied if I do not dominate. I can be proud of my performance and celebrate my growth, but until I dominate, I will not be content!

Either dominate or fail. In most classes in school, you are given a letter grade (A–F). Every so often, you have a course where there are only two possible grades—pass or fail. As you approach your underdog dreams, do so with a dominate-or-fail mentality. Either you dominate or you do not pass and must do better.

IT AIN'T OK TO JUST BE OK!

You can't have excellent goals and have mediocre standards for yourself. Excellent goals will require that you first set excellent standards for yourself. You must meet those standards before you can ever achieve those goals.

OVERTIME

Long before people of excellence pursue greatness, they establish a personal standard of excellence for themselves. The standard, which is simple and absolute, is that anything less than your best is unacceptable. While the masses who do not subscribe to such an extreme standard will accept good and maybe even great effort, people of excellence won't. Instead, they believe that 99.9 percent is not good enough, and there is no wiggle room. Either they do their best and give their all, or they fail miserably. It matters not the external result. They could have scored 30 points in a game, been the highest-performing employee at work, won a Grammy, or had the entire world applaud them. But if they knew deep down that they did not give their all, they'd be disappointed with themselves.

LEMON DROPS

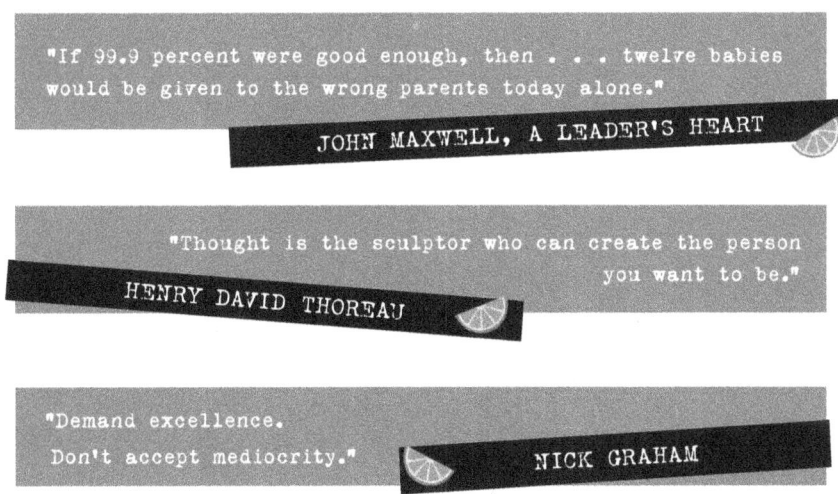

"If 99.9 percent were good enough, then . . . twelve babies would be given to the wrong parents today alone."
JOHN MAXWELL, A LEADER'S HEART

"Thought is the sculptor who can create the person you want to be."
HENRY DAVID THOREAU

"Demand excellence. Don't accept mediocrity."
NICK GRAHAM

5. ESTABLISH AND PROTECT YOUR STANDARD OF EXCELLENCE – 1ST HALF

Challenge | Understanding | Preparation | Accountability

As a competitor, there's no worse feeling than the failures you could have avoided had you been properly prepared. The pain and regret for such losses hit differently. If we are honest with ourselves, we have all been there. Sitting in an empty locker room after an avoidable loss, an empty house after an avoidable breakup, an empty office after an avoidable termination, an empty room after being replaced in the starting lineup—whatever it is, that burns and is indeed an empty feeling.

My most memorable avoidable failure came during my sophomore year as a college hooper. As a competitor, I had established excellent standards for myself. I pushed myself in practice, never took reps off, did morning workouts, made extra shots after practice, moved heavy weight in the weight room, and stayed disciplined socially during the season, attending parties only if the next day was a day off.

At the time, I was not playing much. But because of my standards of excellence, I was productive and efficient in practice. That led my coach to frequently assure me that my hard work was not going unnoticed and that if I kept working and stayed patient, opportunities would come my way. His affirmative words kept my spirit encouraged.

Games came and went, but my situation remained the same. Finally, just as I began to seriously doubt if I would ever break into the playing rotation, the coach called me to tell me I had made the playing rotation! He apologized and explained that he should have played me much earlier and that my spot in the rotation was long overdue. He assured me I would begin playing at least half of the game and be the first guard off the bench.

After that phone call, I felt validated, appreciated, and grateful that my established standard of excellence would finally pay off. Our next game was about a week away on the road against the #1 ranked team in the country. My commitment to the grind was leveled up even more before that game. This was well worth the wait! Not only was I getting an opportunity, but I was getting it on the big stage and under the bright lights against the best team in the country. A few hours before the game, my coach called my hotel room to make sure I was ready for my delayed but well-deserved opportunity. He again assured me that I was the first guard off the bench. With 100 percent conviction, I told him I was ready to go.

Early in the game, one of the starting guards committed his second foul. If one of our guards picked up two fouls in the first half, they were done playing until the second half. Despite giving me his word, the coach chose to put another player in. We ended up losing by more than 20 points. Coach decided not to give me the meaningful minutes he promised. Instead, he inserted me into the game with less than a minute left in the second half.

I learned the hard way that we must protect our hope at all costs. Because I was competitively immature and emotionally weak, that encounter led me to lose hope, which caused me to lose my drive—and I'm not proud of that. When I lost my drive, my goals became unattainable because my standard of excellence was now non-existent. No longer was I first in sprints, going hard in the weight room, staying late to get extra shooting, and going to bed early to be well rested. Instead, because I lost hope, I went through the motions in practice and did just enough to get by. I coasted in the weight room, and instead of being the last one to leave practice and staying late to shoot, I left practice as early as possible so I could go out and overindulge in my social life. As a result, both my confidence and conditioning decreased significantly.

ESTABLISH AND PROTECT YOUR STANDARD OF EXCELLENCE – 1ST HALF

A few weeks later, we were back on the road playing another nationally ranked team. We were playing so badly that our coaches emptied the bench, hoping to find players who cared enough to play with competitive pride and passion. Previously I would have been able to deliver, but because I had allowed my external circumstances to lead me to abandon my excellent standards, I was awful when the coaches put me in. I was so out of shape that after running up the court only a few times, I felt like I had just chain-smoked a box of Newport cigarettes. Needless to say, my performance was poor.

In the locker room after the blowout loss, our coach provided each of us with a tailor-made butt-chewing. He went right down the line and undressed us all. When he got to me, he said, "And you, Nick! Don't you ever come to me and b#*%h about playing time again! You asked for a chance, and you got it tonight. That was your last chance!"

As much as he pissed me off and as much as I felt he had previously done me dirty, he was right. I had no one to blame but myself. Had I been competitively mature enough to protect my hope and hold on tightly to the standards of excellence I established, that would have never happened. As I sat in a dark corner of the locker room, I made a promise to myself and have since stayed true to it. I promised I would never be unprepared for an opportunity again, and I would make sure of that by never allowing an external circumstance to affect my internal standard of excellence again.

HALFTIME

Jim Rohn once said, "It's important to learn from your mistakes, but it is better to learn from other people's mistakes, and it is best to learn from other people's successes. It accelerates your own success." We should all take heart of Rohn's words. Let's learn from our mistakes and other people's successes. More than likely, you will experience the same thing I did. But unlike me, protect your standard of excellence at all costs!

Detach your hope from anything external. The immature me allowed things I could not control to change what I had control over in my competitive standards. Circumstances will be temporary if you approach them properly. While they may feel permanent, they will change, and they will change you for the better if you stick to the standards of excellence you've established. Don't allow your temporary circumstance to become a permanent problem.

LEMON DROPS

"Excellence is never an accident. It is always the result of high intention, sincere effort, and intelligent execution; it represents the wise choice of many alternatives - choice, not chance, determines your destiny."

ARISTOTLE

"I often say 'Pursue excellence, ignore success.' Success is a by-product of excellence."

DEEPAK CHOPRA

6. ESTABLISH AND PROTECT YOUR STANDARD OF EXCELLENCE – 2ND HALF

Support | Hope | Endurance | Accountability | Nourishment | Understanding

Another memorable underdog moment came when I was a college athlete. It was my junior year after I made the promise to myself in the locker room to never be unprepared for an opportunity again. I was riding the bench, and nothing seemed to change that no matter how hard I worked. As I lay on my bed in my dorm room, angered by my athletic situation, I could not even sleep. So I made an underdog vow to myself. I vowed to let go of the hate and dominate what I could dominate. It was my way of controlling my controllables.

Like any committed underdog, I looked at myself in the mirror and acknowledged I had no control of the coach, whether he would put me in the game (my hate). But I could control whether I worked on my game harder than anyone else, played harder than anyone else, ran sprints harder than anyone else, and prepared harder than anyone else. I told myself that since I was not in the playing rotation, I would approach practices like they were my game day. The internal standard by which I measured each drill, sprint, and moment was that either I dominated or I failed. There was no in-between.

While my teammates were in the locker room before practice, casually listening to music, joking, and capping about what girls were shooting their shots at them, I approached practice like it was the national championship game. By the time the others arrived on the practice floor, I was already drenched in sweat, mentally prepared to dominate.

During our early practice drills when the norm was to work our way toward game speed, I was already going full throttle. When running sprints, instead of just making the time, I was trying to lap everyone. I refused to take a water break. I accepted that I was an underdog and did not have reps or time to waste.

During games, I'd get to the gym so early that I had to get up shots in my street clothes because I was at the arena before the managers were. When the other players came down for shots, I was already focused and ready to go. That continued for weeks, and I had yet to touch the floor. Night after night, I'd cry myself to sleep—hurt, angry, mad, and even bitter. But more than anything, I was determined. The more I was ignored, the more determined I got. Through this process, I learned that underdogs are often invisible until the stage is set for them to be visible.

When you are invisible to your coach, your coworkers, your talent agent, or whoever else has yet to see what you are destined to become, you can get mad, frustrated, and cry yourself to sleep. Don't stop working, and don't stop believing that you will get your chance.

I remember asking a manager to rebound for me before a game. That was part of their job description, but the manager just laughed and refused. He explained that since I wasn't getting in the game, he had more beneficial things to do with his time. In practice, I would take a charge—brace myself for the opponent who had gained momentum to run me over, which forced a turnover and drew a foul on the opponent—and no one would help me up off the ground. No coach would pat me on the back or give me a fist pump. I was in my invisible stage. But because of my underdog oath, the more I was invisible, the more I doubled down on dominating through my newly established spirit of determination.

After weeks of invisibly dominating, we played a big game against a nationally ranked team. I did my regular pre-game routine and again reminded myself of my underdog oath—let go of the hate and dominate what you can dominate! As fate would have it, the starting point guard turned his ankle. When he did, I got up off the bench and looked at my coach. My body language screamed, "Put me in the game if you want to win!"

That worked! It's as if my coach had an out-of-body experience and without thinking put me in the game. The starting guard was not severely hurt; it was just an ankle tweak. That meant they would retape his ankle, give him way too much ibuprofen, and throw him back in the game. I would get back to rotting away on the bench.

It would take less than five minutes to examine his ankle and retape it, which meant my window of opportunity was small. I was operating with little to no margin of error. In the face of that, I still thrived! The source of my success was the underdog mindset I had developed. It led me to accept that the underdog journey was an uphill climb, and that produced my underdog determination—an uncommon conviction in your ability, even in the most disadvantageous circumstances.

I was so effective in the small window that by the time the starting point guard got his ankle taped, the coaches couldn't take me out of the game because of my productive play. We went from being down eight points to being up by 15. After the game, everyone showered me with love—even my coach who was dishonest, overlooked me, and didn't give me a fair shot to play. Even the manager who blew me off because I was a bench-warmer not worth his time; and everyone else on my team was praising me. They respected me for my performance, but most importantly, they respected me for my response to not playing.

That moment prepared me for the many underdog battles I've had to fight since. I still hold tightly to the mantra that got me through—let go of the hate, and dominate what you can dominate. I hope you do the same. When you do, it will show the haters and doubters around you that we underdogs are often invisible until the stage is set for us to be visible!

OVERTIME

Don't allow your sight to affect your vision—the anticipation of what may come. You may see a coach that does not think you are good enough, a boss that will not promote you, social media talking heads speaking bad on your name and discrediting your ability.

But maybe it's what you don't see— the coach dismissing a favorite player who plays your position or a player's injury, and now you're the starter (that's how Tom Brady got his first NFL start). Maybe it's a crisis within the company you work for, and you are the one best equipped to solve the problem. Out of desperation, they reach out to you. Or after frequently being overlooked, you're introduced at your favorite coffee shop to a gorgeous woman with a pretty smile and a pure heart (that really happened to me). Don't let what you see or don't see affect your vision—what you hope for and believe about your future.

Just because you do not see your next opportunity does not mean it's not lurking around the corner. Often, opportunities are senseless and will surprise you and pop up out of nowhere. So when you're so discouraged by your temporary circumstances and tempted to lose hope, don't. When it surprises you, you need to be prepared. When opportunity arises and surprises, get rid of the hate, dominate, and hold tightly to your established standard of excellence.

LEMON DROPS

"I believe in destiny. But I also believe that you can't just sit back and let destiny happen. A lot of times, an opportunity might fall into your lap, but you have to be ready for that opportunity. You can't sit there waiting on it. A lot of times you are going to have to get out there and make it happen."

SPIKE LEE

"You may have to fight a battle more than once to win it."

MARGRET THATCHER

"Strength does not come from winning. Your struggles develop your strengths. When you go through hardships and decide not to surrender, that is strength."

ARNOLD SCHWARZENEGGER

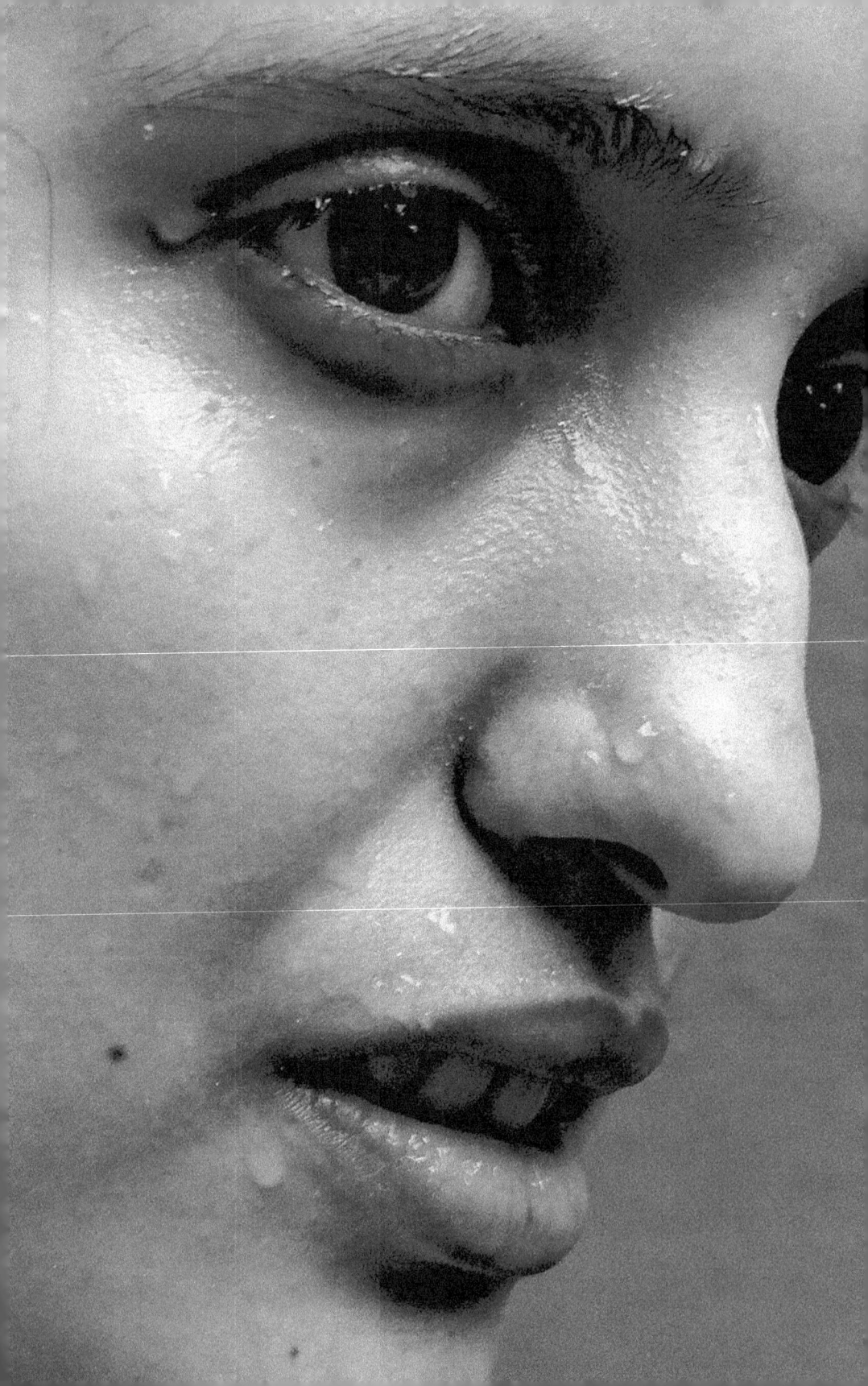

7. ERIC GARCIA: BEING THE PARTY > ATTENDING THE PARTY

Prioritization | Perspective | Hope

Most if not all of us suffer from FOMO (fear of missing out), whether socially, professionally, competitively, or fashion-wise. Of course, this mainly relates to social media. Most assume FOMO holds us back, but I'd argue that it doesn't have to. If we pivot our perspective, FOMO could be the driving force that pushes us toward our potential in all we pursue.

Eric Garcia's story is one of my favorites. He is currently a pro basketball player. As Underdog E, he scratched off all the items on his basketball bucket list. He wanted to be one of the top players in the state as a high school player. Check! He got a D1 basketball scholarship. Check! He wanted to be a difference-maker at the D1 level. Check! And he wanted to be a pro ballplayer. Check!

Not only did Underdog E reach his goals by maximizing his basketball potential, but he also actually exceeded them. As a college player, he pushed past simply being a difference-maker and was one of the best point guards in the school's history. He started as a freshman and led his team to a conference championship and an NCAA tournament berth. As a professional, he's the lead guard for a league championship team and is one of the top players in the entire league.

Early on in Underdog E's high school career, he was "slept on." Despite being the hardest-working player around, no one assumed he would ever be good enough to play at a high level. This is a common occurrence for underdogs along their journey to greatness.

To overcome the hate and doubt of others, Underdog E doubled down on his commitment to his dream. The extra effort and time he put toward his basketball dream created a FOMO fork in the road. There were many Friday nights when he was in the gym with me instead of going to the party, or if he did go to the party or the football game on a Friday night, he'd have to leave early because we had an early morning shooting session or boxing workout the next day.

As Underdog E checked his Instagram feed or Snapchat and saw his friends appeared to be living their best lives at a pool that was litty, on vacay, or at a raging party, he would question whether his sacrifice was worth it. But eventually, his hard work did pay off, and he got his D1 scholarship. He had earned his scholarship, but now he had a lot of work to do if he wanted to play as a freshman. His coaches expected him to redshirt or be a bench-warming backup his first year.

As hard as Underdog E had worked to get his scholarship, he would again find a way to work even harder and sacrifice even more, which once again created a FOMO fork in the road for him. As he continued to grind, the question lingered. Is this really worth missing out on having an elite social life? That friction led Underdog E to a breakdown in the middle of a workout, and I abruptly ended it early.

That would be the first and last time we would ever prematurely end a workout. We went to our favorite restaurant, Pappadeaux, and ordered everything on the menu because I was paying. Then Underdog E courageously told me, "Sometimes I feel like I am missing out on life and that I just want to be a normal kid."

I heard E and understood him, but I also understood why he worked so hard. At that moment I asked him, "Do you work hard to be normal?" He, of course, responded, "No." I then provided him with an affirmative yet accurate peek into what his future could look like. I told him I thought he was good enough to start as a freshman in college and that he could make money hooping after college. I then asked him if he believed he could have such a future. He replied with an emphatic "Yes!"

After Eric was convinced of the possibilities of his basketball future, he had the proper perspective concerning what he was afraid to miss out on. He correctly concluded that he was more fearful of missing out on living out his childhood dreams of being a big-time college basketball player and professional hooper than he was about missing out on the upcoming late-night kickback or extended beach vacay.

Before Eric's conference tournament championship game on ESPN to advance to March Madness, he called me. We meditated and celebrated in the moment. I informed him that all the "normal kids" back in Denver were going to be partying, and while he again could not attend the party, he was the party as there were watch parties all over the city to see him shine on the big stage! I then asked him if he still felt like he was missing out on being "normal." Eric laughed, got off the phone, and went on to lead his team to a championship.

As you digest Underdog E's story, remember the definition of an underdog—a competitor who appears to have little to no chance of winning the fight. Frequently throughout Eric's underdog journey, others thought he had little to no chance to win.

An underdog must be a fierce, frequent, and fearless competitor. If this had not been true in Eric's case, he would have never reached and exceeded his goals. The same holds true for you.

OVERTIME

How dope is Eric's story? He feared missing out on the party but continued to sacrifice and stand on his dream. And then he became the party!

LEMON DROPS

"When a person can't find a deep sense of meaning, they distract themselves with pleasure."

VIKTOR E. FRANKL

"The road to success is dotted with many tempting parking spaces."

TRADITIONAL PROVERB

"I'm a great believer in luck, and I find the harder I work the more I have of it."

THOMAS JEFFERSON

8. CHECKMATE

Support | Hope | Affirmation | Empowerment

The day after signing my scholarship, I woke up early, eager to read the feature story in the local newspaper about my signing. It included quotes from my mother, high school coaches, and future college coach, which is standard for such an article. The quotes are most often congratulatory in nature, which was the case with my high school coaches and mother. However, my future college coach (let's call him Coach Davis) was not as positive as I had hoped.

While Coach Davis expressed excitement about my joining the team, his primary focus in the interview was to announce that he would redshirt me. This was news to me since it was never mentioned previously. In college athletics, coaches can redshirt a player for one year, meaning the player will practice and develop but will not be eligible to play in games. That is often done if a player is injured or the coach believes the player is not ready to immediately contribute. The article quoted Coach Davis as saying that while I possessed the talent, I was too small, too weak, and too little to play as a freshman in a "grown man's league like the Pac-12 conference."

I signed my scholarship in April, and our first game was not until November. While I agreed that I was not ready to battle "grown men" in April, I had six months to get stronger. Even though I had time to develop, Davis had already decided before I got on campus and practiced with my teammates that I would not play as a freshman.

Coach Davis's comments disappointed me, but they did not discourage me. Tony Gaskins once said, "Work in silence and let 'em sleep on you. The noise from your success will wake 'em up in due time." That was my energy during the six months before our first game. While Coach Davis was busy telling the world how weak and fragile I was, I silently leveled up. Instead of lifting with my high school team, I reached out to the Oklahoma State University football strength coaches and asked if I could join their off-season workout program. They allowed me to join, but there was one condition. If I slowed them down, I had to quit on site. For four months as an 18-year-old underdeveloped kid, I kept up with world-class athletes—or should I say grown men—many of whom would go on and play in the NFL.

When I reported to campus in July, Davis expected to see yesterday's me. Instead, he saw a version of me he never assumed I could become. I'll never forget walking into the weight room the first time. With intention, I walked in wearing an extra tight Nike Dri-FIT tank top to show off my gains! Everyone's jaws dropped because I looked nothing like the small, skinny high school kid I used to be. My new teammates were impressed at my build and how "college-ready" my body was. One of the seniors on the team and the team comedian, Ced, yelled to Coach Davis, "Coach, you full of s&%t! I don't know what the hell you was talking 'bout saying he's too small to play with grown men. He pulled up in here like he's fresh off a bid [in prison]." When we did our strength testing, my max bench was 260 pounds, the second-strongest among guards. Because of the strength I developed, I was not redshirted and played as a freshman. Checkmate! Keep quiet, and know that one day when you win, you too will yell "Checkmate!"

Unfortunately, many people in your life—like Coach Davis in mine—will label you solely on what they see and make no consideration for what they can't. It seems appropriate to circle back to the definition of an underdog. Remember, it is one who appears to have no chance of winning. It's not that we underdogs aren't capable. It's just that an inaccurate assessment has been made of our ability based solely on our current exterior appearance with no consideration for what can't be seen—the soul and spirit of an underdog. It's what can't be seen that qualifies underdogs to win, which explains the frequent inaccurate underdog assessments.

Hold on to this thought as you continue your underdog journey. You must never allow another person to label you. Labels limit us. If we are honest with ourselves when we have accepted the label others have placed on us, it limits what we can become and achieve. Hosanna Wong captures this incredibly by stating, "When we answer to the wrong names, we live out the wrong stories." Wong further explains, "The false stories we believe about ourselves can trap us into the wrong living patterns." That is why every underdog must know the difference between fixed and growth mindsets.

The underdog soul and spirit that can't be seen leads us to compete with a growth mindset instead of a fixed one. Fixed mindset competitors do not continually level up. They are satisfied with yesterday's version of themselves, which is why who they were yesterday is who they are today. It's why who they are today is who they will always be.

But the opposite is true. For growth mindset individuals, leveling up is a lifestyle. Yesterday's version of them stays in yesterday. They relentlessly pursue a better version of themselves with every day they live, every breath they breathe, and every rep they take. That is why underdogs will always be so much more tomorrow than they appear to be today.

OVERTIME

An underdog's statement of faith in their future self: Because of the growth mindset within me, I am incapable of being the same me tomorrow that I am today. When others inaccurately predict what I will achieve in my future based on today's version of me, I will refuse to accept that limited label and won't answer to that name. Instead, I will move forward knowing there is no limit to what I can become as long as I move forward and stay committed to always being better than yesterday's version of myself.

LEMON DROPS

"Move in silence, only speak when it's time to say checkmate."

— UNKNOWN

"Individuals who believe their talents can be developed (through hard work, good strategies, and input from others) have a growth mindset. They tend to achieve more than those with a more fixed mindset (those who believe their talents are innate gifts)."

— CAROL DWECK

"Ships don't sink because of the water around them. Ships sink because of the water that gets in them. Don't let what's happening around you get inside you and weigh you down."

— UNKNOWN

9. SKIP THE SKIPS

Support | Affirmation | Hope | Mental Health
Blocking out the Noise

I heard this a long time ago, and it stuck with me:

- 25 % of the people in your life don't like you and never will.

- 25% percent don't like you, but when you are trending up, they'll rock with you (clout chasers).

- 25% like you, but when you fall off or fall back from the limelight, they will fall back off of you (also clout chasers).

- 25% will ride or die with you, staying ten toes down no matter what. Those are a rare breed, your real ones, your root encouragers, your *committed friends*.

In 2020 during COVID-19 when the NBA completed the remainder of its season in the bubble they created at Disney World in Florida, one of my all-time favorites, Dame Lillard, was named MVP of the NBA's bubble. Sports commentator Skip Bayless has been given the nickname "the diabolical hater," and if you are a sports fan, you will agree that his nickname fits. Despite Dame being named MVP, Skip disapproved of him, refused to acknowledge his MVP, and made it known that he was not impressed with his performance. On his way to earning MVP, Dame had a stretch with two 40-point games, a 50-point game, and a 60-point game. On top of that, Dame's historic scoring efforts changed the trajectory of his team's playoff hopes.

Going into the bubble, Dame's squad, the Portland Trail Blazers, appeared to have no chance of (think underdog) making the playoffs. With the season winding down, Dame and the Blazers' margin for error was almost non-existent. While facing near-impossible odds on the biggest stage, Dame did the unimaginable and led his team to the playoffs. The next day, on *Undisputed*, Skip Bayless's platform to hate on Dame and many others, Skip criticized and dismissed Dame's achievements. He went so far as to say that one of Dame's clutch three-point shots should be dismissed because it was not a swish. Like I said, his nickname "the diabolical hater" fits him. He's a straight hater!

We can learn a lot from Dame, our underdog role model, and how he handled Skip's hate. Dame identified who his target audience was. Clearly, there was nothing Dame could do to get Skip's approval. So because Skip was not a part of Dame's audience, Dame could give two you-know-whats about Skip's opinion. Skip kept hating, and Dame kept winning.

In our lives on and off the court, we all have a Skip. Since social media is a prominent part of our culture, the Skips have more access to hate than ever before. I—and maybe you as well—have been guilty of being influenced by a Skip. There were times when I was living life like "bubble Dame," in my zone positively impacting young hoopers in my community, serving others by providing free workouts, looking to help and encourage others when they were down, and so on. Yet, the Skips always showed up, looked past the good I was doing, and dug deep into nitpicking about something they disapproved of.

That used to bother me! As you've probably experienced, when you know you are wholeheartedly attempting to do good, there's often an audience of haters that will not acknowledge the good you're doing. Striving to please the wrong audience can be extremely deflating. Moving forward, we must not be bothered by the audience of haters who give us their two cents, even though we never asked for it.

Shortly after Dame's bubble run, I had to unleash my inner Dame and prepare to skip the Skips in my life. Before my first book was published, my publishing company warned me that many books fall significantly short of their potential because the writer writes to please everyone. The publisher told me that it's impossible to satisfy all readers. They explained to me that I could write the world's best book but there would still be some "Skips" who would never be satisfied. If I wrote to "satisfy the Skips" who would never be satisfied, it would compromise my ability to satisfy my target audience.

Because of that, the publishing company asked me to identify my target audience before I got too invested in writing the book. Once I identified my audience, I only concerned myself with satisfying them, and them only. My publisher also told me that I must be mentally and emotionally prepared to ignore the unwanted tweets, opinions, and comments of my Skips. Because of my publisher's guidance, I went on to write a book that resonated, inspired, served, and was frequently consumed by my target audience.

In Dame's case, Skip Bayless does not sign his checks, pay for him to endorse a product like Adidas does, or give him the talent and ability to get 60. So why should Skip's opinion matter? In my case, I wrote my first book to encourage, relate to, and affirm the souls of hip-hop-cultured athletes, so why would the opinion of an old, close-minded, non-athletic hater—or anyone else who is not my target audience—matter to me?

For Dame, when he balled out in the bubble, his target audience was overwhelmingly pleased. Adidas, who signed him to a multi-million-dollar contract, was also pleased. His teammates and coaches whom he led to the playoffs were pleased. The millions of loyal fans he has worldwide were inspired and pleased. Teams he competed against respected him. But most importantly, I'm sure Dame, at the conclusion of the bubble, was both proud and pleased with himself.

Once my book was published, my target audience, much like Dame's, was overwhelmingly pleased. The players, parents, and coaches I wrote it for have expressed how it has served them through athletics and beyond. In addition, my publisher shared that my book was rated as one of the staff's best manuscripts that year. And I, too, like Dame, was proud and pleased with what I had accomplished.

Now you! If you have not already done so, skip your Skips. Identify your target audience, and determine if they are pleased with you. As you do, remember what my publisher told me. "It's impossible to satisfy everyone. You could be the best at what you do on the planet. But there will still be 'Skips' who are never satisfied."

If you strive to "satisfy the Skips" in your life who will never be satisfied, you will compromise your abilities to satisfy who matters most—your target audience. Trust that when you do this, like our guy Dame, your haters will keep hating, but you will keep winning!

OVERTIME

You could do everything right, and many may still have an issue with you. You must understand and accept that it's their right to have that issue with you. While that's the case, you must never allow their issue with you to become an issue for you. When you allow another's issue with you to become an issue for you, it will lead you to fight unnecessary and unwinnable battles.

To reach your desired status, there will be fights you must fight and fights you will have to win. Those fights will require everything you have. If you invest your time, energy, and talent in fighting unnecessary and unwinnable battles, it will deplete and discourage you and could be the reason you are not capable of fighting and winning the necessary fights.

LEMON DROPS

"Survived too many storms to be bothered by raindrops."
DAME LILLARD

"You can be the ripest, juiciest peach in the world, and there's still going to be somebody who hates peaches."
 UNKNOWN

"If my critics saw me walking over the Thames they would say it was because I couldn't swim."
MARGARET THATCHER

"Some people will never like you because your spirit irritates their demons."
DENZEL WASHINGTON

10. SWEET FRUITS NEED DEEP ROOTS — 1ST HALF

Preparation | Perspective | Endurance | Support | Challenge
Mental Health

You have no chance to sustain winning without being deeply rooted. As you move forward, I urge you to first subscribe to the mantra that there's no sweet fruit without first developing deep roots! Like a tree that produces frequent, flavorful fruit, we must go down deep in the dirt before we ever come up and blossom.

While this is a simple notion, most are not emotionally mature, prepared, developed, or tough enough to accept four harsh yet necessary truths about growing the deep roots needed to produce what it takes to overcome adversity and adequately handle success.

Truth #1: **When you commit to developing the deep roots needed, your lifestyle won't be Instagram-able!** Developing roots is done in the dark, below the surface, where it's lonely and uncomfortable. Hip hop culture champions the motto "getting it out of the mud." As underdogs, we, too, must not only embrace getting it out of the mud but also commit to living in it because roots dwell in the dirt. And when we live in the dirt, we must be equipped to handle the long periods of dark isolation that come with it.

Our mentality must be different. We cannot be addicted to and driven by the praise, encouragement, and motivation from social media followers or others on the outside. While they'll show us love and associate with us in our fruit-producing stages, those same people are likely to ignore us, disassociate with us, and look down on us when we are grinding through the dirt and enduring the root-developing stage that's needed in order to produce the fruit we love.

Truth #2: **Deep-rooted people prioritize becoming the part, not looking the part.** Becoming the part and looking the part are not the same. Whichever one you commit to will often cost you the other. Obviously, it's much easier to look the part than it is to develop into the part you desire to become. It might be like developing into a pro football player like my friend Karl Paymah, or into an Executive VP like my old teammate Ced Clark. It might be becoming a high-level college coach like Yolett McPhee-McCuin who, as she put it, "really got it out of the mud" as an immigrant from the Bahamas and "came over here and started in junior college and worked her way up." Or it might be growing into a world-renowned content creator like my sister Brittany. Becoming the real thing requires so much more.

Convince yourself that while looking the part is much easier, it's also quite expensive. It might cost you to actually develop into that part.

Steph Curry was trying to convince college coaches and evaluators that he was one of the best players in his recruiting class. Shonn Brown, Steph's high school coach, was frequently told by college recruiters that even though Steph was dominant, they wouldn't recruit him because he didn't look the part. "He's not athletic enough," they said. Because Steph didn't "look the part," he was only rated as the 300th-best player in his recruiting class and had no major scholarship offers.

Hindsight having perfect vision leads us to conclude there are not 300 people who are better than Steph at basketball. While that's true, there were 299 players in his class who "looked the part" of being a better player than he was. Fortunately for Steph Curry, he's a "root guy and not a fruit guy," which led him to commit to becoming the part that all the so-called experts said he didn't look like. His successful underdog climb convinces us that we do not have to look the part to become it. It also validates Truth #1 that when he was dwelling in the dirt, no one was checking for him. However, because he endured, he is now one of the best to ever do it and an underdog role model for us all.

Truth #3: **Deep roots are not developed overnight.** Unfortunately, there will be underdogs who quit prematurely. They will quit because they aren't fully developed in their emotional maturity and toughness. That is why they have subscribed to the social media–centric societal norms that disillusion us to believe that sustained success is microwavable—something that can be expedited, but that's not true.

The success we are after—sustained success of substance—is not what's projected and celebrated on our social media feeds. It can't be sped up, and if an underdog's emotional maturity is not developed, they will never make the perspective pivot to trust that even though the fruit is not yet visible, it will one day be both frequent and flavorful if they continue to invest in deepening their roots.

Because deep roots are not developed overnight, I encourage you to make the declaration that you aren't regular—you are top of the line. That means you cannot develop ordinarily. Look at yourself as a Rolls Royce and not a Toyota Corolla. It takes thirteen hours to build a Corolla; it takes six months to build a Rolls Royce! While there's nothing wrong with a Corolla, we'd all agree that a Corolla is common and a Rolls Royce is top-of-the-line. You too will be top-of-the-line if you complete your root-deepening stage.

Truth #4: **Deep roots have no timetable.** Not only does it take time for roots to develop, but they're also not predictable. That is why perhaps the best underdog advice I ever received was from one of the root encouragers. It was NBA analyst Chris Dempsey who was also gracious enough to write the foreword for my first book. Dempsey kept me encouraged during my root-deepening stage as I wrote that book. He probed me to accept the agreement that I couldn't place a timeline on fruition.

I, like any other committed underdog, am quite ambitious. Obviously, ambition is a required underdog ingredient. But if we aren't careful, our ambition can lead to impatience, which will lead us to become more fruit-focused and less root-focused. Because that's the case, Dempsey's declaration about not placing a timeline on fruition is an essential agreement all underdogs must accept. Instead of putting a timeline on our fruit, we must hold ourselves accountable to diligently, relentlessly, and frequently develop our roots. As we do, much like Steph Curry, we will have faith that our deep roots will one day produce great fruit.

HALFTIME

Power Thought #1: Those whose lifestyle is currently "Instagramable" are either posting an artificial lifestyle or actually got out and endured living in the mud for an extended period of time. Their roots became deep and developed enough to produce frequent and flavorful fruit.

Power Thought #2: Don't get discouraged by people who overlook your roots. They can't see them. Know that the work you put in during the dark and in the dirt will not be witnessed, encouraged, or applauded by the masses. Trust that when your roots are deep enough because you remain ten toes down, then the fruits of your labor will be exposed to the world around you in due time.

LEMON DROPS

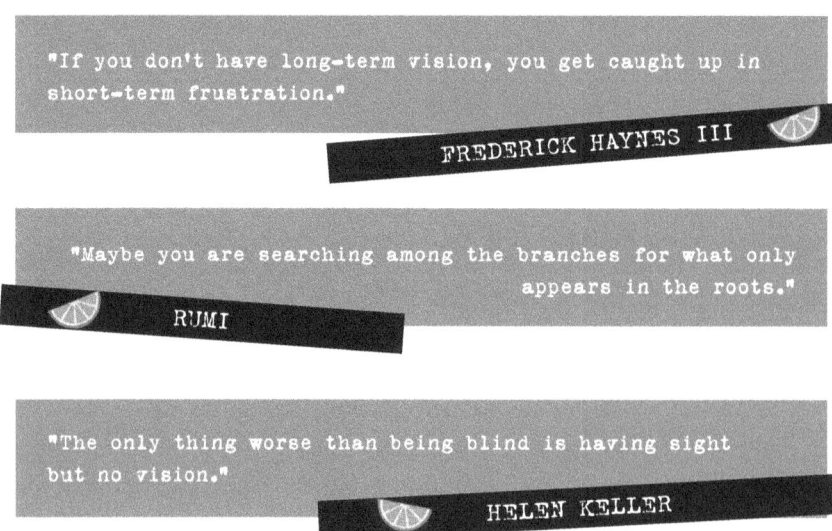

"If you don't have long-term vision, you get caught up in short-term frustration."
FREDERICK HAYNES III

"Maybe you are searching among the branches for what only appears in the roots."
RUMI

"The only thing worse than being blind is having sight but no vision."
HELEN KELLER

11. SWEET FRUITS NEED DEEP ROOTS — 2ND HALF

Preparation | Empowerment | Support

As I mentioned in the first half of these "Sweet Fruits Need Deep Roots" chapters, the masses will not recognize your root development. However, they will praise you after you achieve success. Remember, the real ones in your life are your root encouragers. While we can appreciate the praise from the masses after the fact, we don't need it. It's before and during our root development that encouragement will be the enhanced light we need in order to move through the dark, foggy, hazardous times. We're guaranteed to encounter those times as we commit to developing our deep roots.

As an underdog, we must adhere to what Henry Ford says about obstacles. He said, "Obstacles are those frightful things you see when you take your eyes off your goals." His profound perspective on obstacles is how root encouragers earn their spots on our team. Because we are about this underdog life, we will live life to the fullest and not just survive. That means frequent, heartbreaking, unfair challenges will come. When they do and if they break you down so badly that you temporarily lose sight of your dream and want to give up, it will be your root-encouraging teammates who will come to the rescue and keep your dream alive.

Allow me to tie this all together with a thought about fog lights. On a car, fog lights are used when the standard headlights are not powerful enough to allow the driver to see through the thick, treacherous fog and provide the vision needed to see what's ahead. They help the driver make it safely through the darkness. It's much the same for an underdog. Our root-encouraging teammates provide the fog lights, the extra bright light we need to see our way through the darkest times of our journey. And when we safely make it where we want to go, we'll look back and recognize that if not for those fog-light, root-encouraging teammates, we would have never made it.

Maya Angelou once wrote, "My mission in life is not merely to survive, but to thrive." To live life is to relentlessly go after all of your underdog dreams and desires, no matter how foggy or muddy things get. Yung Pueblo dropped a bar when he wrote, "A clear mission doesn't always have a clear path."

That's why we underdogs must learn how to drive in the fog and maintain clarity all the way. We must be sure our cars have fog lights. Once we commit to driving the underdog's drive and decide to thrive instead of just survive, we must know that our drive ain't no ordinary drive. While our end goal is clear, the drive will be far more treacherous than a non-underdog journey.

Chauncey Billups was a fog light on my journey. He encouraged me while I was completing my first book and doing basketball training in Southern California. He called me one day when my life was definitely "life'n"! I had been knocked down hard, and I was so focused on my challenges that my ambitious and noble goals appeared invisible—in dense fog—and felt unattainable.

Chauncey called to tell me he had just watched James Harden, the reigning NBA MVP at the time, workout with his trainer. He told me to keep going and that despite my current struggle, I had what it takes. He said Harden's trainer was elite but that I needed to know that I was just as good and had a place working with high-level players. When he said that, it was as if my fog lights turned on. While my struggles didn't disappear, the fact that he recognized my deep roots gave me the vision to see through the fog. If Chauncey hadn't called that day, there's a good chance I would have significantly downsized my dream.

Fog
1. a thick cloud of tiny water droplets suspended in the atmosphere at or near the earth's surface which obscures or restricts visibility
2. something that obscures and confuses a situation or someone's thought processes

Fog Lights
1. a bright light on a motor vehicle, used in foggy conditions to improve road visibility

OVERTIME

If you have not already, ensure your roster is primarily of root encouragers.

Take time to give your root encouragers their well-deserved flowers.

I will take advantage of this opportunity to do the same. I hope that along with acknowledging my squad, it also convinces you of how essential root encouragers are along your underdog journey. I would have given up writing my first book and walked away from my passion for teaching basketball and mentoring athletes if not for my root-encouraging teammates.

How foolish would a driver be if they were driving through the thickest fog during the darkest drive and they didn't use their fog lights? Their car is equipped with fog lights, but they chose not to use them. It's the same as going through a dark, foggy drive along your journey and choosing to continue without activating your root encouragers. I will honk my horn and encourage you to turn on your fog lights!

LEMON DROPS

"I always wanted to be somebody. If I made it, it's half because I was game enough to take a lot of punishment along the way and half because there were a lot of people who cared enough to help me."

ALTHEA GIBSON

"Recognize the difference between friends of convenience and friends that are committed. Friends of convenience are a dime a dozen, but committed friends are both rare and valuable."

ANONYMOUS

"A clear mission rarely has a clear path."

YUNG PUEBLO

"Caring friends multiply your joys and divide your pains."

FREDERICK HAYNES III

12. THEY AREN'T PREPARING ON THE SAME LEVEL – 1ST HALF

Support | Understanding | Perspective

A young player I mentor, we'll call her Mia, sought me out to guide her through a frustrating season. She was one of the most hard-working, committed, consistent, passionate players I'd ever worked with at her age. She came from a working-class family with blue-collar values. As a seventh grader, Mia shoveled snow throughout the night during the winter to pay for her basketball team travel and training. She once attended an 8:00 a.m. workout with me after only a few hours of sleep because she was shoveling until 4:00 a.m.

You'd think Mia's coaches would applaud, support, respect, and reward her commitment to excellence, but that was not the case. Instead, which is often the case at her age, Mia played for a team coached by the fathers of two of her teammates who both played the same position as Mia.

Unfortunately for Mia, the coaches were committed to playing their daughters no matter what. Not only did they play their daughters, but they also refused to coach Mia for fear that if they did, she would outshine their children. Instead of coaching her, they chose to magnify her failures and ignore her successes, even though her successes far outweighed her losses.

Mia, who was in tears, passionately told me that they (their daughters) never get yelled at, and they always get coached and acknowledged for what they do well. Mia had 11 assists in their game, and the coaches said nothing. But when Mia made one turnover, they yelled at her and told her she was not good enough and needed to work harder on her own. When she asked them what she was doing wrong, they never gave her an answer.

"It's not fair," she said. "Why is it easier for them and they get rewarded, but I outproduce them, outwork them, and even outcare them? Bro, after games we lose, they don't care. But when we lose, I'm bothered! It hurts, man! So I look at myself in the mirror and figure out what I need to do better to ensure we win next time. It makes no sense, bro."

My response both surprised and frustrated Mia. I replied with a "back-in-the-day" story about when I was addicted to video games. I could sense her "what does that have to do with me and my problem" energy, so I encouraged her to stay with me, and I encourage you to do the same. Let's move on to the second half of this story.

HALFTIME

Mentally join me in the underdog locker room and grab some refreshing lemonade as we break down the first half and prepare for the second.

In sports, halftimes are used to not only recover but also to make adjustments to the opposition. As we compete as underdogs in life, we too must adjust to defeat the opps!

As an underdog, chances are you have either been in a similar situation to Mia's or you will be. If you have and you mishandled it, give yourself grace. Don't beat yourself up. Instead, learn a lesson. In Dr. Chérie Carter-Scott's book *If Life Is a Game, These Are the Rules*, my favorite of her ten rules is this one: "There are no mistakes, only lessons!"

And here's the lesson. As underdogs, we must be mentally and emotionally prepared to overcome unfair and unjust agendas of supervisors, coaches, teammates, and coworkers. While Mia's frustrations and yours in similar situations are valid and it's healthy to recognize them and vent to your competitively mature and emotionally healthy root encouraging supporters, you cannot allow these obstacles to stop you or even slow you down!

Consider this. Your haters are nothing more than an obstacle. Choose to keep your eyes on your goal. By doing so, you won't be bothered by obstacles because what you don't see can't bother you. And since your eyes are on your goal, you won't run from obstacles. Instead, by running toward your goal, you will overcome all challenges in a way that will not compromise your character!

LEMON DROPS

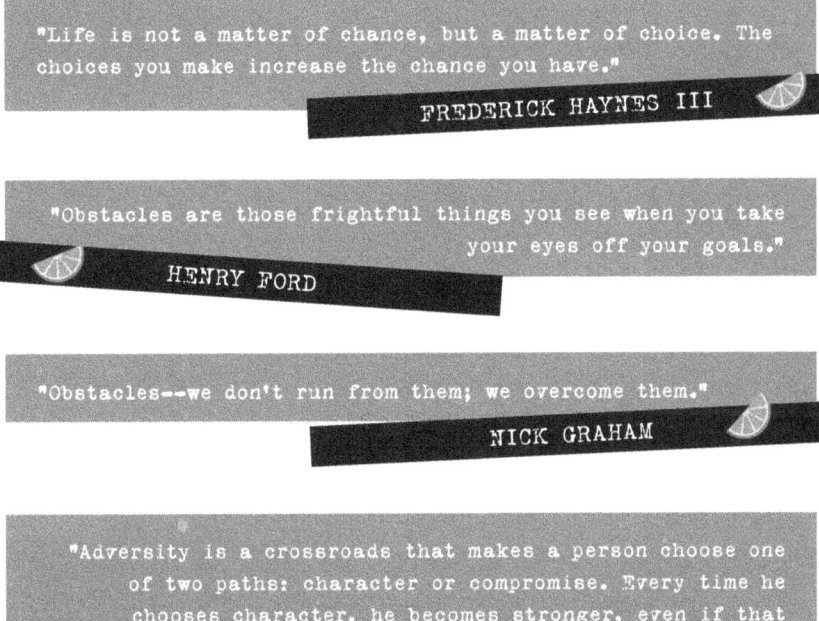

"Life is not a matter of chance, but a matter of choice. The choices you make increase the chance you have."
— FREDERICK HAYNES III

"Obstacles are those frightful things you see when you take your eyes off your goals."
— HENRY FORD

"Obstacles—we don't run from them; we overcome them."
— NICK GRAHAM

"Adversity is a crossroads that makes a person choose one of two paths: character or compromise. Every time he chooses character, he becomes stronger, even if that choice brings negative consequences."
— JOHN MAXWELL

13. THEY AREN'T PREPARING ON THE SAME LEVEL – 2ND HALF

Endurance | Resilience | Encouragement | Empowerment
Affirmation | Nourishment

Before I had to grow up and retire my controller, I was known as one of the best NBA 2K players on the block! In fact, I was so good that I was a first-ballot NBA 2K Hall of Famer! During those days, my cousin Daniel ("D"), who was nowhere near as passionate about 2K as I was, had never lost in 2K! Not only did he not lose, but more times than not, he also won by at least a dub (more than 20 points).

I rarely frequented the "dub club," and I also took my fair share of losses. If I am going to keep it all the way real with you, a few times I was the one on the wrong side, the receiving end of the "dub club" as I got beat by 20. As I compared my turbulent path of close games, losses, and getting dubbed to D's display of dominance and perfection, I got mad, frustrated, discouraged. And if I'm honest, I'll admit I even got a little jealous of my li'l cousin D.

Here I was putting in work on the 2K playground, playing online against the best of the best, and playing in career mode. In contrast, D sporadically played yet was dominant. When D played, he was on the phone, reclined back, casually playing. My phone was off when I played, and I was upright at attention, locked in and alert like the serious guy on the popular video game meme! It just did not seem fair.

For some reason, D would never connect with me to play head-to-head. Something was always off. First, his Internet went out. Then he said he didn't want to play online so he could deliver my L in person. Then, when I showed up at his house, he had homework he "forgot about."

Once we finally played, I beat the breaks of D. I smacked him by 30 points the first time. After that, we ran it back three more times, and every time we did, I lived comfortably in the "dub club" with at least 10 points to spare as I beat him by more than 30 points all four times. It was so easy for me that I turned my phone on, made a call, and reclined back. As I did, I glanced over and saw D at attention, locked in. He wasn't on his phone any longer. Truth be told, he couldn't even use it because he cracked the screen after the second game when he threw it across the room in frustration. After the fourth loss, Lil' D wanted no smoke with his big cousin and never played me in 2K again.

I'm sure you're wondering how I went from getting dubbed and taking losses to making D wave the white flag and quit because I was beating him so badly when he had been winning so easily. Here's what I found out. Lil' D's dad, Uncle Larry, told me that D had been playing on rookie level! He was winning there, and I was getting crushed on the Hall of Fame level. For those who know nothing about NBA2K, the rookie level is the easiest level where you can dominate without being challenged. By contrast, the Hall of Fame level is the most challenging level where even if you are a promising player, you can still get crushed. I chose to play on Hall of Fame to prepare for my upcoming challenges, and Daniel lived on rookie. When we met, I dominated him even though he had never lost on rookie.

As you continue to have the courage to prepare at your Hall-of-Fame level, remind yourself that while those preparing on rookie may be winning now, they aren't working on the same level. Keep your head down, stay on the grind, and trust that your Hall-of-Fame preparation will produce dominant results.

THEY AREN'T PREPARING ON THE SAME LEVEL – 2ND HALF

OVERTIME

Think of yourself as a grape that is more than capable of reaching its potential of becoming the finest wine. What separates a grape from its potential and the desire to become fine wine is the crushing process. While most grapes avoid the pain of the crushing process at all costs, other grapes will endure the temporary yet painful process of being crushed in order to reach their potential. And you, the underdog, are no different! You can't become who you want to be and do what you want to do without going through a crushing process or two. Keep going!

LEMON DROPS

"The longest way is a shortcut."
— ANDREA MASCHIG KRENEK

"The underdog journey is an uphill climb."
— NICK GRAHAM

"Hardships often prepare ordinary people for an extraordinary destiny."
— C. S. LEWIS

14. GEORGE CONDITT IV: PROGRESS PRECEDES PROMOTION

Acceptance | Empowerment | Encouragement | Mental Health
Resilience | Hope

As a competitor, current professional basketball player Underdog George is living his best life. Over the past year and a half, he was a team captain on a Sweet 16 team, represented Puerto Rico in international basketball competitions, signed a good-paying professional basketball contract, and led his professional team to a league championship. Most recently, he played on national TV against Team USA composed of NBA All-Stars. He held his own, scoring 12 points and grabbing six rebounds! George is literally living out all his competitive dreams.

While George is living it up now, his story was far from sweet. As recently as a year and a half before, George, while still a college player at Iowa State, was in a dark, depressed place, both as a competitor and as a person. He was overweight, discouraged, unmotivated, and athletically speaking canceled on social media. His team, which had a tradition of winning, was historically bad, and George as a basketball player wasn't very good. If I am being honest, he was hot garbage. As I tapped in to watch him play on ESPN, he looked like he did not belong and did not want to be there.

To say George had lost his way along his competitive journey would be a vast understatement. I respected George's competitive space and kept my thoughts to myself. However, after George's third or fourth conference game, I couldn't take it any longer and reached out to him in hopes of assisting him in finding his way back to being the hard-working, energetic, hopeful, passionate, and confident player and person he used to be.

After hearing George's heart and allowing him to listen to mine, George was encouraged. He began to take small steps toward rediscovering his hope, passion, and enthusiasm. Now reinvigorated, George's next game was a prime time Saturday night nationally televised contest against Oklahoma. While our pow-wow of positivity comforted him, at the end of the day, it would take far more than a pep talk for him to experience on-court wins against future NBA players.

George had previously abandoned his aggressiveness and hadn't been playing in attack mode. He was now back to being aggressive George. He posted up hard and yelled for the ball. When they passed it to him, he made one of the most decisive moves I'd ever seen him make. He attacked hard middle, but the defender cut him off. George reacted by spinning off the defender and into a beautiful jump hook. It was elite!

George's defender, an athletic shot blocker, was beaten. Still, his wingspan and ultra-athleticism allowed him to recover and block George's shot into the third row. The home crowd went crazy. George's coaches threw their faces into their hands, and some of George's teammates were visibly frustrated. George made the highlight reel on ESPN for the wrong reasons. They showed it from multiple angles, three or four times, even in slow motion, and showed the shot blocker flexing to the crowd afterward.

When I had seen George make the move, I jumped out of my chair and yelled excitedly at the TV. "Good move, boy!" I was enthused because when I saw George make that move, I knew he was on the road to living his best life as an athlete. So I texted him. "Big time move, my boy!" George question-marked my text and said, "Bruh, what you mean? He beat my shot into next week, lol."

I then sent George a slow-motion replay of his move before the shot, along with a few NBA players making a similar move. I also sent him

GEORGE CONDITT IV: PROGRESS PRECEDES PROMOTION

clips from his previous games when he looked like hot garbage. George recognized that his move looked similar to NBA players and that his aggression and swag when he had the ball in his hand were much better than in the previous games. As I encouraged George for his progress, I made sure he understood that his coaches and teammates were frustrated with him because they were so consumed with the end result that they could not recognize his vast improvement. That's not shade toward his teammates and coaches because if I'm 100, I would have reacted the same way. However, I assured him that a perspective pivot would be needed. He would need to have a different mindset than his teammates and coaches. His new attitude had to be that he focused more on his progress and less on the end result.

I assured Big George that while it may take a while, if he focused on the progress within the process, the result would eventually change. I told him that most aren't emotionally tough and mature enough to endure the negative results. Still, I was challenging him, being the underdog he was, to be built differently. George bought into the pivot and began developing more confidence and hope in his ability and future possibilities. By the end of the year, the same guy getting dragged on X, formerly known as Twitter for being washed, was now going toe-to-toe with some of the top players in the country.

George carried that same energy into the next season and was a starter on a team that went from winning just two games the previous season to 22 the next. Because George became consumed with committing himself to improvement, his end result gradually began to improve, which is how he went from playing like hot garbage to overcoming his darkest times athletically and eventually becoming a pro hooper.

Learn from Underdog George. Just because the end result is not yet what you desire, it does not mean you are not incrementally improving and inching closer to your desired goal. After George's team upset Wisconsin and advanced to the NCAA's Sweet Sixteen, he Face-Timed me from the locker room. He said with tears and a winning smile, "Graham, we did it, bro! And to think this all started with me getting my sh*t tossed to the cheap seats."

As you digest George's triumphant underdog story, consider if there is an area in your life where you have been blinded to your progress because the outcome is not yet what you desire. As you do, remind yourself it could be worse! At least you did not get your shot blocked into the cheap seats on Sports Center like George. If he can keep his head up, be proud, and recognize his progress after that, you can too. Keep going, underdog!

OVERTIME

What should not be overlooked in George's story was that he allowed his adverse circumstances to lead him to abandon his aggressiveness and no longer play in attack mode. Once he did that, his production spiraled. On the other hand, once he was competitively mature enough to be aggressive and attack regardless of the circumstance, he began to dig out of his competitive hole. If we aren't careful, as we continue on our underdog quest, we too will allow losses and failure to lead us to stop being aggressive and living in attack mode. Instead, we must trust that circumstances are not permanent; they will change. Like George, when we commit to remaining aggressive and continually attacking, our discouraging competitive circumstances will change for the better.

LEMON DROPS

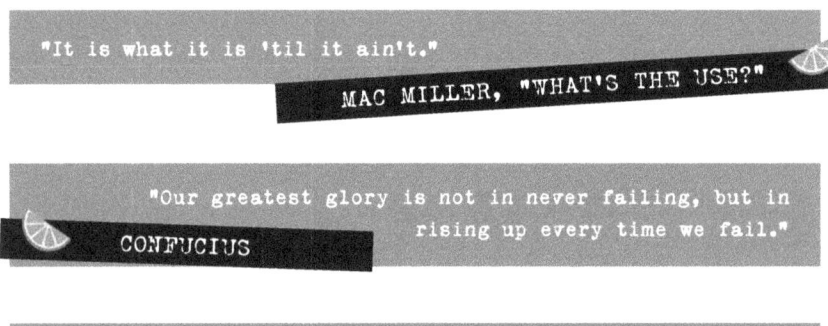

"It is what it is 'til it ain't."
MAC MILLER, "WHAT'S THE USE?"

"Our greatest glory is not in never failing, but in rising up every time we fail."
CONFUCIUS

"You can't let praise or criticism get to you. It's a weakness to get caught up in either one."
JOHN WOODEN

15. GORGE CONDITT IV: RECIPE FOR OVERCOMING COMPETITIVE DEPRESSION

Acceptance | Empowerment | Encouragement | Mental Health Support | Hope

At the root of George's athletic depression he was losing his joy. When I called him, I first asked, "What do we need to get you back to being happy?" Like most athletes and competitors, George was taken aback by my question. He had never had someone in the competitive space ask him about his happiness, and he was not prepared to answer.

Over the next hour, George Conditt IV and I developed a six-step process to help him find his joy and overcome his competitive depression. Being the courageous underdog he is, George wants you to enjoy the lemonade from the lemons of his life. He wants me to share that six-step process.

1. **Look at yourself in the mirror (and keep it 100 with yourself).**

No different than in hoops, you can't attack what you don't confront! The way you attack competitive pressure with an aggressive and confident face-up, you must do the same with life.

Face your struggle, and acknowledge the lessons you need to learn. *The Rules for Being Human tells us there are no mistakes in life—only lessons. Lessons will keep repeating until we change our behavior.

2. 🍊 **Find the joy you lost
   (and this time, get below the surface).**

George's decline was because he allowed his circumstances to rob him of his joy. Once he lost his joy, it directly and harshly impacted his on-court performance. I challenged him to find the joys of basketball that were below the surface and had nothing to do with results and performance. No more surface joys!

George dug deep and rediscovered his deep joys for playing basketball. They were joys that had nothing to do with notoriety, stats, playing time, or any other external factors. George rediscovered these joys:

- Being part of a team and playing for something bigger than him.
- Remembering that basketball games were organic family reunions where his parents, siblings, grandparents, aunts, uncles, and cousins all came together to watch him play. Whether he won or lost, they'd all break bread together after the game.
- Developing a brotherhood with his teammates.
- Competing at the highest level against the best of the best.
- Being challenged.
- Sharing the thrills of winning with teammates.
- Overcoming the pains of defeat with teammates.

Once George thought about his below-the-surface joys, I suggested that those joys drive him. Since they were internal joys and no one or nothing gave him those joys, no one or nothing had the power to take them away. So he could compete with a spirit of joy regardless of his external circumstances.

3. 🍊 **Remind yourself who the hell you are
   (and convince yourself that you are still that person).**

Once George's performance began to decline, his swag evaporated. I reminded him of how dope, confident, and talented he was. I assured him that despite the fact he was in a slump, he was still that dude or he would have never made it to that level in the first place. I YouTubed some of his old mixtapes from high school and convinced him that he's still "like that."

After I flooded our text threads for a week with highlights, he began to remember who the hell he still is and was convinced *he* was still *him*.

* Being *him* or being *her* is simply being a successful underdog—one built to win the fights they say you can't, one that can handle all the smoke thrown your way!

4. 🍊 Be realistic!

It's going to be a marathon. It took you a long time to dig yourself into this hole, so it will take you a long time to dig out of it. Build your mental and emotional endurance.

This is by far the most challenging step. This is also the fork-in-the-road step that breaks many. They'll listen to Eric the hip-hop preacher, Inky Johnson, or any other motivational speaker, and then they're ready to run through a brick wall. They read and state positive affirmations and meditate, and then they're ready to go into battle. That helps them apply pressure for a day, maybe even a week, but at some point, they become discouraged and are overwhelmed with how much work still needs to be done and erroneously assume they are failing.

They attempt and expect to journey a thousand miles in a day (more on that in Step 5). When George was at Step 4, I made sure he understood that it would not change overnight. I told him he was not going to show up for the next game and go from playing six minutes and averaging two points and one rebound to getting monster double-doubles. I made sure he knew he was signing up for what inspirational NBA player Isaiah Thomas calls the "slow grind." All he needed to do was take one step in the right direction each day.

5. 🍋 **Celebrate small victories.**

The journey of a thousand miles starts with a single step.

Celebrate each step! Winning breeds winning, and when you get on a mental or emotional winning streak, you will increase your expectancy of winning.

When you accumulate a large quantity of small Ws, you will carry that energy into more challenging situations and develop the habits and mindset to be prepared to get some bigger Ws. Next thing you know, you'll be eating Ws left and right, like Jameis Winston!

George began to dig himself out of the hole when he celebrated his small victories. He even celebrated in the midst of adversity when he made an aggressive move that resulted in getting his shot blocked into the third row! While this was not the desired result, he still acknowledged and celebrated the fact that he made his most aggressive move of the season, which encouraged him to continue his aggressiveness. He gradually improved and eventually was back to getting buckets on the regular.

I suggested that George keep a daily journal. I suggest you do the same. In this journal, give yourself at least six compliments, and list at least 10 small victories every day. By becoming aware of your small victories and positive attributes, you'll begin to convince yourself of who you are—*him* or *her*!

6. 🍋 **Record your recipe, and replicate it!**

I stole a page out of Mama Graham's cookbook. Anyone who knows my mother knows she is one of the best cooks on the planet. Family members have driven down from other states just to eat a few pieces of her sweet potato pie! After years of indulging in her pie, I was in the kitchen watching her prepare it for the first time.

I was surprised to find her intently studying her recipe. I figured after all these years of making pie so good it makes you want to slap yo' mama that she was a pro and no longer needed to follow her recipe. That prompted me to ask her why, after these years, she was still intently following her recipe.

She quickly put me in my place and said, "Being that I love to bake, the holidays are my Super Bowl. When everyone enjoys my food, that's my championship MVP moment. Over time, through my experiences, I have established and recorded a recipe that guarantees success. So why on God's green earth would I ever leave that to chance?"

In George's journal, I encouraged him to continually identify, record, and follow his recipes of success so he, like Mama Graham, would increase his chance of replicating success.

OVERTIME

After our conversation and game plan, George later told me that he "felt like a huge weight had been lifted off of him." He also explained that he felt comforted and hopeful because we had a mental and emotional game plan to win the mental battles. That makes sense. Competitors, whether athletic, corporate, or otherwise, have grown accustomed to depending on a game plan to thrive. Since that's the case, I encourage you to not only follow in George's footsteps but to do so much earlier.

George waited until two-thirds of the season passed to allow me to serve as his mental and emotional competitive coach. That meant he played over half the season with a crippling emotional-mental weight that significantly slowed him down. To overcome, we must approach mental and emotional support just as we do physical support. Could you imagine Steph Curry shooting poorly and waiting until half the season passed to seek support from his shooting coach? Of course not! It's the same when we seek mental and emotional support.

George did the work and deserves the credit because it was not easy, and it was not instantaneous. Like any caring coach, all I did was accept, support, and empower George, as well as hold him accountable. The same is true for you. As you courageously identify safe people in safe spaces to coach and support you, you must commit to doing the emotional and mental work.

LEMON DROPS

"You can't heal from what you won't deal with and ain't real about."
FREDERICK HAYNES III

"Still I'll rise."
 MAYA ANGELOU

"Vulnerability sounds like truth and feels like courage. Truth and courage aren't always comfortable, but they're never weakness."
BRENÉ BROWN

"Happiness can be found even in the darkest of times, if one only remembers to turn on the light."
J. K. ROWLING

"I will be patient with myself as I develop into the person I am meant to be. Being perfect is not the goal. Continuing to grow in a positive direction is the goal."
 UNKNOWN

16. AGGRESSIVELY PURSUE EXCELLENCE, NOT PERFECTION

Perspective | Encouragement | Support | Empowerment | Hope

Me: When you're watching SportsCenter and they highlight the game's top performer, is that Player of the Game the most perfect player?

Ryan (team player): No.

Me: At the end of the season when they award the league's top player, are they acknowledged as the MPP for Most Perfect Player or MVP for Most Valuable Player?

Dixon (team player): MVP, Coach.

Me: Are teams awarded trophies and rings for perfection or being a champion?

Cole (team player): For being a champion.

Me: So you're telling me that for a competitor to reach their goals and be their best, perfection is not a required ingredient in their winning recipe?

Brady (team player): No, it's not, Coach.

Me: While perfection is unnecessary, do you think all the scenarios I mentioned require excellence?

Eli (team player): Absolutely, Coach!

Duncan (team player): Yeah, Coach, for sure!

Me: Do you think you can achieve competitive excellence without aggressively pursuing your goals?

Fritz (team player): Nah, Coach, you can't.

Me: You guys understand that the more aggressive you commit to being, the less likely you will be perfect, right?

Hutch (team player): I never thought of it like that, Coach, but it makes sense.

Me: So why are you guys pursuing and demanding perfection of yourselves when it's not required to get us where we want to be? Not only that, but by expecting perfection, you guys are abandoning aggression, which we've just agreed is needed to excel as a competitor.

Team: *crickets*

That's how the post-practice conversation went with the Valor High School team after our first practice during summer training camp. They were between coaches, and I was asked to coach them for their summer season. When most competitors work with me for the first time, they aren't mentally and emotionally prepared for the frequent failures that await them. It often results in shaming themselves for the uncharacteristically high volume of failures they encounter during a 90-minute practice.

While it's true that the Valor High School team failed frequently, they also improved dramatically, mainly because they attacked the practice with maximum aggression. In fact, they improved more in the next 90-minute session than in the four workouts I'd observed the week before. Because of their improvement, I was pleased, proud, and feeling good about their chances to reach their collective and individual potentials for the upcoming season. They had taken the

AGGRESSIVELY PURSUE EXCELLENCE, NOT PERFECTION

first step in establishing and committing to a standard of competitive excellence.

My post-practice talk continued.

Me: You guys played with maximum aggression all practice. I am both proud and pleased with your effort. If you all compete like that, you will reach your potential.

I want you guys to know this is a safe space to aggressively fail. As long as you give your all and commit to learning from every mistake, I won't be mad. I'm not looking for the perfect player, the perfect game, or the perfect practice.

Now that I have given you guys permission to fail, I need you to also give yourself permission. The more you do, the more you make way for the most aggressive version of you to take permanent residence!

Drake (team player): Bet. Coach! We got you!

Hutch (team player): Maximum aggression! We with it, Coach!

Duncan (team player): Yep, Coach, we will do that.

Me: From here on out, let's make this team declaration: "We will be the most aggressive, competitive, toughest, and resilient team on the floor every time! If we do that, we will live and learn, which means we can live with and learn from the result, which will allow us to be better for the experience."

Chet (team player): Yes sir, Coach!

My guys at Valor honored our declaration. We didn't win every game, but we did excel, and each player was the best version of themselves as a competitor.

OVERTIME

We're all going to fail, but don't let failure shame you. Be proud of yourself. Recognize your resilience, and celebrate your successes. Remind yourself that your journey does not require you to strive for perfection, which robs you of your aggression. Commit to being aggressive as you pursue excellence. While you do that, you'll be giving yourself permission to fail so you can courageously compete!

I invite you to accept the underdog declaration my li'l bros at Valor High made, Be the most aggressive, competitive, toughest, and resilient competitor every time! And when you fail, live with that and learn from it.

Always remind yourself of the underdog agreements about excellence, perfection, failure, and aggression.

- Excellence and perfection are not the same.
- Striving for excellence is demanding, challenging, and uncomfortable. It requires supreme sacrifice, but it is attainable. And no matter how hard you grind, how much you sacrifice, and how hard you are on yourself, perfection is most often unattainable.
- It's competitively healthy to demand excellence from yourself. At the same time, it is competitively unhealthy, unrealistic, and debilitating to place the unrealistic expectation of perfection on yourself.
- Whether you commit to excellence or expect perfection, the results are not guaranteed. But when you commit to excellence reaching your potential is.
- Stop believing the lie others may be telling you—that you need to be perfect to reach your potential.

AGGRESSIVELY PURSUE EXCELLENCE, NOT PERFECTION

LEMON DROPS

"You may encounter many defeats, but you must not be defeated. In fact, it may be necessary to encounter the defeats, so you can know who you are, what you can rise from, how you can still come out of it."

MAYA ANGELOU

"Perfectionism is a delusion that can rob one of a very successful, enriching life if not careful."

APRIL BRYAN

"Perfection is a roadblock to progress."

UNKNOWN

"The most valuable thing you can make is a mistake. You can't learn anything from being perfect."

ADAM OSBOURNE

17. KNOCK KNOCK: OPPORTUNITY – 1ST HALF

Preparation | Nourishment | Resilience | Excellence

Life-Changing Opportunity: Knock knock.

Underdog: Who's there?

Life-Changing Opportunity: Opportunity.

Underdog: Yes! It's about time! Opportunity, I have been waiting for you my entire life! Hold on, let me go get my shoes, and then I'll be ready! (Leave to go put shoes on and get prepared to leave.)

Underdog: (Comes back to the door, ready). Opportunity, you there? Where'd you go? I don't see you. (Underdog calls Opportunity's phone.)

Life-Changing Opportunity: (answers phone) Hello. Opportunity speaking.

Underdog: Opportunity! This is me. You just knocked on my door. I told you to hold on so I could get ready to go. I came back to the door after I was ready, and it appears you left. Where ya at?

Life-Changing Opportunity: I did leave. The thing about me is that I am impatient, and I am rude. Because of my impatience, I refuse to wait, so when I knock on your door, you'd better be ready to go. And because I am rude, I usually don't let you know when I am coming. I just pull up on you unannounced. Sorry, but that's just how I roll.

Underdog: Wow! I didn't know that about you. Will you ever come back?

Life-Changing Opportunity: Who knows? Sometimes I circle back and visit again. Other times I just pass through. And if you answer the door and you're ready, you can ride with me. If not, I'll just move on to the next door. Since you are an underdog, there's a good chance I won't come back. I know it's unfair, but I rarely visit underdogs twice, so you and all the other underdogs had better be ready when I knock.

I was fortunate to coach underdog Cody. He was a college athlete recruited by the previous coaching staff. The current staff didn't think Cody was good enough to play at our level, which resulted in the higher-ups on the coaching staff deciding not to invest any time in developing him. I was in charge of designing an on-court development program for each player. When I met with our head coach (let's call him Coach Rogers), he told me what he wanted me to improve with each player. When we got to Cody, he told me to not even waste my time because he would never play one second of meaningful basketball for us.

To say Cody was dealt a lousy hand would be an extreme understatement. Could you imagine going to work every day with a team-first attitude, going above and beyond what's expected of you, and in exchange for your loyalty and hard work your coaches or supervisors refuse to coach you, teach you, encourage you, correct you, or provide you with any sort of feedback? Unfortunately, that was the hand Cody was dealt.

Cody was from Texas, like me. We played for the same AAU team. He also went to the same church as my Aunt Carolyn—my number-one fan (every underdog needs one). Her belief and support of me were unwavering, undeserved, and unconditional. Without her being my ride-or-die, I would not have been coaching in college. As you know, I'm a proud member of the underdog gang, so when Rogers told me not to waste my time coaching Cody, an underdog rage erupted within me. There was no way I was going to bypass the opportunity to coach a fellow underdog. After discovering he was from my home state and knew the president of my underdog fan club, my Aunt

KNOCK KNOCK: OPPORTUNITY – 1ST HALF

Carolyn, I knew I had to go against Rogers' wishes and coach Cody up. If I didn't, Aunt Carolyn would reach down and smack some underdog sense into me.

After practices, Cody and I snuck back into our practice facility to put in nightly, no-nonsense, blue-collar underdog work. As we continued our nightly grind, I knew Cody trusted me, and I felt obligated to keep it 100 with him and let him know that Rogers vowed he would never play. Underdogs are often playing against a stacked deck, and to give Cody a chance to win, he needed to know what he was up against. He needed to know that if opportunity came knocking, it would not knock twice.

I told Cody that he had a chance because of his underdog DNA. During practices, I frequently pulled Cody to the side, pulled my shirt up over my mouth like Lebron, and authoritatively whispered that he was fighting an unfair fight. I told him that even though he was working hard, he had to empty his clip, dig deep, and find a way to work even harder.

As the season started, Rogers stayed true to his declaration, and Cody did not play any meaningful minutes. Despite being a bench warmer, Cody's energy to do the extra work with me every night was undaunted. Then out of nowhere, Knock Knock! With no warning, opportunity knocked! We were in the semi-finals of one of the ESPN Thanksgiving tournaments on the biggest stage, and our guards were getting torched. If nothing changed, we were going to lose a winnable game. However, if we could find a spark, we would push through and advance to the championship game. Rogers was so desperate that he put Cody in the game.

Let's just say Cody's shoes were on and tied tight when opportunity came knocking! He balled the hell out. Rogers was praying for a spark, and Cody gave him fireworks—4th of July fireworks. Rogers assumed he would throw Cody in the game and have us coaches calm the guards down, give them a pep talk, and get them back in. He was just hoping Cody wouldn't go in there, piss down his leg, and embarrass us until he got the other guys back in the game. But Cody played so well that Rogers couldn't take him out of the game. Cody finished with 21 points. He was the Player of the Game. He was the reason we advanced to the championship game. And then we went on to win that marquee Saturday night ESPN game.

The media swarmed Cody for interviews after the game. But before that, Rogers had acknowledged Cody in front of the team and said how proud he was of him—with good reason. The same guy he swore would never play for him just saved his bacon!

After the interviews, Cody and I embraced. His parents gave me a big hug and thanked me for not giving up on their son. And for Cody, having Coach Rogers look him in the face man to man in front of his teammates and recognize his talent and hard work was one of the most rewarding feelings he'd ever experienced. His underdog work ethic and attitude had earned him that feeling.

OVERTIME

An underdog is a competitor who is thought to have little chance to win a fight—so they say!

LEMON DROPS

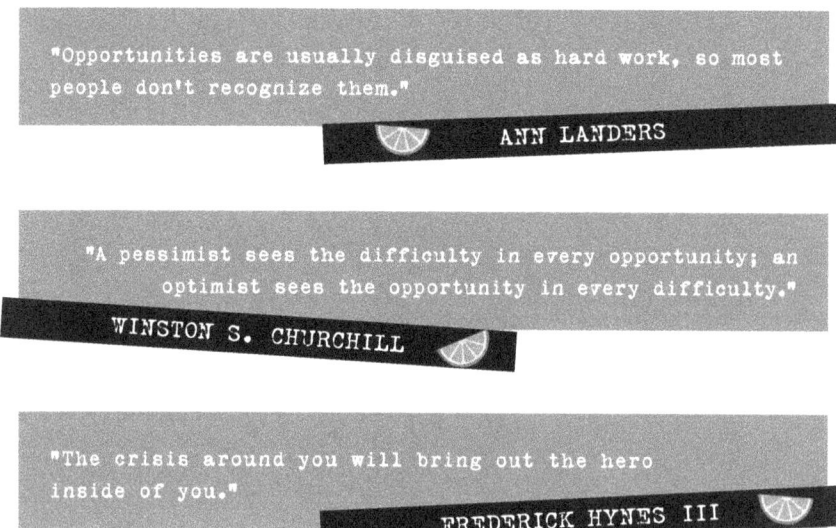

"Opportunities are usually disguised as hard work, so most people don't recognize them."

ANN LANDERS

"A pessimist sees the difficulty in every opportunity; an optimist sees the opportunity in every difficulty."

WINSTON S. CHURCHILL

"The crisis around you will bring out the hero inside of you."

FREDERICK HYNES III

18. KNOCK KNOCK: OPPORTUNITY – 2ND HALF

Preparation | Perspective | Empowerment | Mentality | Challenge

Since underdogs can't count on getting multiple opportunities to reach their goals, they must be great at the wait. I was training current pro and former NBA first-round lottery draft pick Ekpe Udoh a few summers ago. I was scheduled to work out De'Andre, a high school player, immediately after that. After Ekpe's workout and since he is such an overachiever, he wanted to get some extra work in. So I had him make five swishes followed by four in a row from seven different spots from NBA three-point range. Ekpe's extra work caused De'Andre's workout to start later than expected. De'Andre had aspirations of being one of the top players on his high school team, and to make that happen, he had to improve his ball handling, his change of speed, his strength and conditioning, his jumper, and his IQ.

De'Andre's mother dropped him off at the gym 20 minutes before his workout. While he waited, he chose not to work on ball handling, footwork drills to work on his speed, or core exercises to address his lack of strength. He chose not to watch the game film to develop his basketball intelligence. Instead of addressing what he needed to develop and reach his goals, he threw on his hoodie, popped in his AirPods, went to a dark corner, sent a few Snaps, and fell asleep.

It took Ekpe 15 minutes to finish his extra shooting, which meant De'Andre had 35 minutes to wait. Since De'Andre was just 15 years old and still figuring out life and what it means to be a competitor, he didn't realize how vital waiting is and had not yet developed effective waiting habits. I explained to him that he must dominate his wait in order to reach his potential. I had him audit how much time he had waited over the last month and what he did with that time. He quickly realized that the 20 minutes early that his mom had dropped him off, the 20 minutes he had after a workout waiting for his dad, and the unexpected 15 minutes before his workouts started added up over time. Yet he had nothing to show for his waiting time.

De'Andre has since committed to dominating his wait. At one of our later workouts, he again had to wait because Ekpe was getting in some extra work. After Ekpe's workout finally concluded and I was ready for De'Andre's workout, he was already drenched in sweat and breathing heavily. During the wait, he had worked on his change of speed and footwork. Shortly after that, the trajectory of De'Andre's basketball career rapidly ascended. He finished his summer season strong and was projected to be a role player off the bench for his high school team. Because of his unexpected and accelerated improvement, he ended up starting for his high school team and was selected as an All-Conference player.

Later, De'Andre called to thank me for demanding that he dominate his waits. He said that if he hadn't effectively waited, he would have never been prepared for his upcoming opportunities. As mentioned in the 1st half, we never know when opportunity will knock on our door and how long it will wait. It would be in our best interest to be productive during any kind of waits in life or unexpected disruptions. Are you going to be the old D'Andre or the new one?

OVERTIME

Even when it feels like opportunity will never come knocking and you are waiting forever, keep dominating. Maybe you're at an entry-level position. If that's you, while you wait, take those courses, learn those skills, and ear hustle on the coach's or exec's conversations.

Dominate your wait like my old teammate Ced Clark. He went from entry-level to senior executive at Walmart. Like Ced, your opportunity's coming!

Dominate your wait like current Ole Miss Head Women's Basketball Coach Yolett McPhee-McCuin! Coach Yo, as she's known, is one of the most respected coaches in the game, but before her shine, she was a Bahamian immigrant who became the first ever Bahamian woman to coach at a D1 college. Like Coach Yo, your opportunity's coming!

Dominate your wait like my former basketball client Charles Smith. Charles continues to level up. He was daring enough to move to Los Angeles to pursue his dream. He worked odd jobs, took multiple acting classes, auditioned for every role he could, and as a result, got roles on mainstream television shows such as *Snowfall* and *9-1-1*. Like Charles, your opportunity's coming!

Maybe your heart desires to find the person of your dreams, get married, and have an amazing family. While you wait, keep striving to become the best version of yourself, refuse to compromise your standards, and surround yourself with the right people. Dominate your wait like two of my favorite people, Grant Trout and Madi Prewett-Trout. I met Madi and Grant around the same time, but they hadn't yet met. They met a few months later and are now happily married! Both of them had dominated their waits and then found the person they would fall in love with.

LEMON DROPS

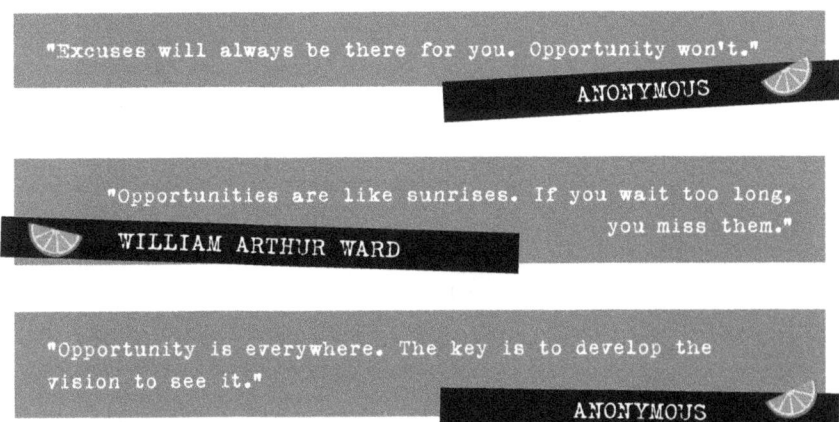

"Excuses will always be there for you. Opportunity won't."
— ANONYMOUS

"Opportunities are like sunrises. If you wait too long, you miss them."
— WILLIAM ARTHUR WARD

"Opportunity is everywhere. The key is to develop the vision to see it."
— ANONYMOUS

19. UNDERDOGS, ACTIVATE

Preparation | Perspective | Endurance | Passion

Usually it's not underdeveloped talent that's the root of a competitor falling short of their potential. It's most likely an underdeveloped competitive mentality. In Chapters 5 and 6, "Establish and Protect Your Standard of Excellence," I mentioned that I was crushed competitively when my coach lied to me about getting more playing time. It compromised my internal competitive standard of excellence, which eventually caused me to compete with a mediocre mindset.

Once the mediocre mindset took over, it affected my on-court performance, and my hopes of earning more playing time were dead. That would never have happened if I had been fully developed mentally for competition. But unfortunately, I wasn't fully developed because I never activated.

I learned firsthand the importance of activation from my friend Melvin Sanders. I learned most of it at his gym, SandersFit, where Mel provides cutting-edge strength, movement, and mobility performance training for elite prep, college, and professional athletes. He currently works with NBA and NFL players Derrick Henry, Buddy Hield, Seth Curry, and Dak Prescott, to name just a few.

The first phase of Mel's workouts is dedicated to activating. Mel explained that whatever muscles are worked during training must first be activated. According to Mel, athletes are subject to injury when muscles are not activated before strenuous use.

I was able to jump in and join one of All-Pro and NFL rushing champ Derrick Henry's off-season workouts with Mel. After 15 minutes of hard work, Derrick and I were out of breath and drenched in sweat. We assumed that what we had experienced was part of the actual workout. But to our surprise, it was just the activation phase. As we struggled to catch our breath and grab a quick sip of water, Mel said, "Now that we are properly activated and prepared, we are ready for the real work!"

Mel then explained that the workout called for a lot of stress and strain on the muscles we were working, so our activation phase was going to be more intense than usual. Actually, it might have been harder than the workout!

As we—any of us—prepare to achieve excellence in the competition of life, athletics, healthy relationships, business, and beyond, we must make sure from a mental standpoint that our toughness, resiliency, consistency, focus, and belief in our ability despite the adversity we battle are properly activated beforehand. If not, like me in the "Establish and Protect Your Standard of Excellence" chapters, we are subject to allowing external discouragement to damage us internally. As underdogs, we must subscribe to the anonymous quote, "Ships don't sink because of the water around them. Ships sink because of the water that gets in them. Don't let what's happening around you get inside you and weigh you down."

Applying Mel's activation stage to our competitive journey requires us to adopt the mindset of NBA player Ja Morant who emphatically stated about his team, "We climb up the chimney. We ain't duckin' no smoke." While most avoid smoke, we underdogs, as Ja said, go out of our way to look for challenges. By looking for obstacles that most avoid organically, we successfully enter our activation stage. In that stage, even if we fail, we fully develop our underdog DNA, which equips us to never fold, never doubt, and always overcome.

And here's our go-to underdog mantra, in Nelson Mandela's powerful words: "Difficulties break some men but make others. No axe is sharp enough to cut the soul of a sinner who keeps on trying, one armed with the hope that he will rise even in the end." That and our

Morant-inspired mentality allow us to develop the internal standard of excellence and resilience.

So remember this when your coach is capping like mine and your teammates have yet to see the greatness within you and won't swing the ball in your direction. Remember it when you're not one of the good ol' boys or girls at your job and were overlooked for the promotion despite putting in twice as much work as everyone else. While it may disappoint you, it will not discourage you, and it won't prevent you from pushing through to the other side.

OVERTIME

Have you matured as a competitor? Mature competitors understand that although the activation phase may be painful and exhausting, they can't avoid it. If they do, permanent harm is likely. We must develop our own mental activation exercises to ensure that we will be mentally and emotionally prepared for the competition ahead.

External adverse factors such as hate, failure, manipulation, misjudgment, injustice, and being overlooked will not break my underdog soul because I have allowed my mentality to fully activate beforehand. The underdog soul within me is far greater than anything the world can throw at me!

LEMON DROPS

"Challenges make you discover things about yourself that you never really knew."
CICELY TYSON

"Good luck is a residue of preparation."
JACK YOUNGBLOOD

20. DAYLEN KOUNTZ: TOUGH TIMES DON'T BREAK, THEY CREATE

Support | Encouragement | Hope | Nourishment | Resilience

Underdog, before you move forward, you must pivot your perspective regarding how you feel and approach your toughest times. The pivot is that your most challenging times are not meant to break you but are sent to create the best you. It's common for ultra-successful achievers to acknowledge, as they reflect on all they have achieved, that without the difficult days they spent at rock bottom, the current success they are experiencing would never have come to be.

That was the case for underdog Daylen Kountz. He was a supremely gifted basketball player who came out of high school ranked as a four-star (out of five) recruit and the top prospect in Colorado. Because of all he achieved in high school, Daylen expected to build on his accolades and hit the ground running in college at the University of Colorado.

As a freshman, Daylen averaged 18 minutes and 5 points per game and occasionally made SportsCenter's highlights with his emphatic dunks. Considering he was on an experienced team with two future NBA players who were also guards like Underdog Daylen, the fact that he could contribute at all was impressive.

Since he had a positive freshman season and had accomplished so much in high school, Daylen expected to be that dude his sophomore year. He expected to take a massive step toward his lifelong dream of becoming a collegiate star and then a professional basketball player.

Unfortunately and unexpectedly, Daylen's sophomore year did not go according to plan. He began the year as a starter but continually struggled. Over the year, he averaged just 12 minutes and 3 points per game. As the season progressed, his minutes and production rapidly decreased. Throughout the last 11 games, he averaged only 4 minutes and 0.9 points per game.

Daylen's turbulent second season sent him into a dark, depressive state. As an athlete, he hit rock bottom. It was his Mandela fork-in-the-road moment. This dark, difficult time would either break him like most athletes, or he would tap into his underdog DNA and refuse to allow his soul to be broken. Daylen was hurt, angry, confused, and had lost his athletic swagger. He shared with me that his swagger was at 1,000 going into college, but when he hit rock bottom during that brutal 11-game stretch, his swag vanished and fell to zero.

The kid that once was certain he'd be a pro ball player was now considering quitting and going to get a 9 to 5. Despite his discouraged (but not broken) spirit, Daylen chose to keep showing up. He shared, "When I was at my lowest, I finally reached a point when I was able to keep it real with myself and decided to control what I could control, which was working hard, showing up, and getting better every day. No more pouting and feeling sorry for myself. I still was not playing, and it was not sweet, but I convinced myself this was temporary, and while it was tough, I just had to be tougher."

Daylen's decision to not allow his dark days to break him and instead create a better him gave him the foundation needed to thrive when he transferred schools. He averaged 21 points a game, and his shooting percentages increased tremendously. Because of all he had endured, he developed his leadership skills and was selected as team captain. Daylen led his team to win 22 games and an appearance in the conference championship game.

In Daylen's nightmare sophomore season, he played 18 conference games in the Pac-12. In those 18 games, he averaged just 1.5 points per game—that's 28 points total. But at his new school, Northern Colorado, his team played a road game against Arizona, one of the top four teams in the country and the best team in the Pac-12 by far. Daylen played the entire contest, connected on four of the five three-pointers he attempted, made all his free throws, and scored 33 points! In one game against the best team in the conference, he outscored his sophomore season total (18 games) by 5 points, and of course, he had a highlight dunk that was featured on ESPN!

At the time of writing this, Daylen, after being one of the most explosive scorers in college and a first-team all-conference selection, just accomplished his lifelong dream and signed his first professional basketball contract! Daylen's underdog journey shows that when we reach rock bottom, just as he did during that 11-game stretch of his sophomore year, if we go in the right direction when we hit our Mandela fork, we too will not be broken. When he was at rock bottom, he felt it was a sign that he should downsize his dreams or even abandon them altogether. But now that he is on the other side of his dark days, he, like other ultra-successful people, knows that his tough times weren't sent to break but to create. That resulted in him chasing down his big dreams of being a college basketball star and becoming a pro ball player.

Underdog, here's to hoping you choose to be created and not broken by your difficult days.

OVERTIME

Perspective Pivot: Foundations cannot be built from high above. If you are at rock bottom right now, I feel for you. I know how hard, dark, and lonely it is. However, while it's a painful place to be, rock bottom is the place you need to be. You need to be there to build a strong, sustainable foundation to support the success that awaits you in your future.

LEMON DROPS

"Hitting rock bottom doesn't mean you have to stay there."
MICHELLE PARSONS

"What you can become depends upon what you can overcome."
 ANTHONY DOUGLAS WILLIAMS

"Keep in mind, when you hit rock bottom, there ain't nowhere to go but up, baby."
LUDACRIS

"If you have never reached rock bottom, you have never attended the school of greatness."
MATSHONA DHLIWAYO

"When you feel like you have been hit, dig deep and hit back. Rock bottom is not your end; it is your beginning."
 CHRISTINE EVANGELOU

21. DESTINATION-DRIVEN, NOT TRANSPORTATION-FOCUSED

Perspective | Prioritization

Years back, I partnered with an NBA player (we'll call him Leon) to do a basketball camp in our community. We bodied the camp, and most parents, coaches, and players shared with us that our camp was the dopest they had ever attended. I mean, we had everything—free Chipotle, a camp All-Star game, a celebrity game, the dance of the day, a DJ, and of course elite basketball. We even had Denver Nuggets PA announcer Kyle Speller introduce the All-Star game participants the same way he introduces the Nuggets players at home games. To say we were lit would be an understatement.

On the first day of camp, Leon told me he was going to Vegas when the camp was over to watch the NBA Summer League, to unwind, and to start working out for the next season. He suggested I link up with him to celebrate the camp, network at the NBA Summer League, and train him for a few days.

He told me he'd pay me for the workouts and that he had a wraparound luxury suite with a fountain view comped at the Cosmopolitan with $1,000 in free room service. I could have it all to myself. All I had to do was pay for my plane ticket. I immediately booked my ticket and was floating on cloud nine since this was such a rewarding moment for me. All my hard work was paying off, and this was a once-in-a-lifetime opportunity both professionally and personally.

Leon and his close friends left a few days before I did. I had to stay back and tie up loose ends when the camp ended. Leon is a high-roller, and a perk of being a high-roller is that the casinos will comp your travel on a luxury private plane. As I scrolled my social media timelines and saw all my boys having the time of their lives flying private, eating the finest foods, drinking unlimited Topo Chicos, and partying in the friendly skies, I was stuck preparing to fly Spirit. If you've ever flown Spirit, you know it's a major downgrade from flying private! If you haven't, that's great for you, but to feel my pain, google "Spirit Airlines memes," and you'll get it!

For the next 48 hours until my departure, I spent a lot of time looking at social media posts and stories of Leon and his boys flying private. The rewarding and promising destination that once encouraged me was now replaced with comparing transportation, and that discouraged me. My discouragement became a distraction. The time I wasted on social media should have been devoted to shopping so I could look my best. I should have connected with my barber so my cut could be crispy, and I should have watched game film to prepare to train Leon. Because of the time wasted, it was too late to get a cut from my main barber, and I had to settle for a backup barber who was suspect and pushed my hairline back. I did not have time to go shopping and was not clear-minded while watching game film.

Once I landed in Vegas, it was lit! I was VIP at the NBA Summer League and successfully networked with influential people. The suite at the Cosmopolitan was off the chain. I trained Leon, and he was pleased. He picked up the tab at 5-star restaurants, and I even met superstar songstress Kelly Rowland. As I look back on that trip, I realize that once I got to where I was going, how I got there or how anyone else got there didn't matter. All that mattered was that I got there. Not once when I was VIPin' it up at Summer League, ordering surf and turf, chicken 'n' waffles, Sour Patch Kids, and Topo Chico from room service at the Cosmo, or training an NBA star did I ever consider how I arrived in Vegas, nor did anyone else. They did not turn me away at the gate when I showed my VIP credentials at Summer League. They didn't demand that I check out of my suite, and Leon didn't decide not to train with me because I flew Spirit and didn't arrive on a private plane.

DESTINATION-DRIVEN, NOT TRANSPORTATION-FOCUSED

I am sure my experience in Vegas is very entertaining and gave you a good laugh. Still, I am hopeful that as you continue on your underdog voyage, you will do so with the proper perspective. The perspective pivot needed is for you to always keep the main thing the main thing. When my focus was on my main thing, I was floating on cloud nine. But when my focus was on the wrong thing—Spirit Airlines—I saw my guys on their Jack Harlow "flo" flying first class without me, which poisoned my perspective.

That came with consequences. I learned the hard way that when you allow the method of transportation—how you get there—to distract you, you run the risk of not being fully prepared once you arrive at your destination. Since I was so focused on my transportation to my destination instead of being focused on my preparation for my destination, it bit me in the butt big time. I mentioned that I met Kelly Rowland. Well, my fit wasn't fresh, my hairline was crooked, and aesthetically speaking I was not my best self. Because of that I had no confidence to "shoot my shot." Had I been properly prepared for the trip with a positive perspective, who knows—I could currently be Mr. Kelly Rowland.

As you continue on in your competitive pursuits, learn from me, and make sure you're prepared for your destination. And if you happen to meet a Kelly Rowland when you arrive, you'll be your competitive best self!

OVERTIME

Do you remember what Jim Rohn said? "It is better to learn from other people's mistakes." Learn from me not to get so focused on the mode of transportation that you stop preparing for your destination. Be destination-driven, not transportation-focused. Remind yourself that you'd rather take less-than-desirable transportation to your ultimate destination than take ultimate transportation to a less-than-desirable destination, because once you get to where you desire to go, how you got there won't matter. All that will matter is that you got there!

LEMON DROPS

"The only thing you sometimes have control over is perspective. You don't have control over your situation. But you have a choice about how you view it."

— CHRIS PINE

"Life is about perspective and how you look at something . . . ultimately, you have to zoom out."

— WHITNEY WOLFE HERD

"The problem is not the problem. The problem is your attitude about the problem."

— CAPTAIN JACK SPARROW, PIRATES OF THE CARIBBEAN

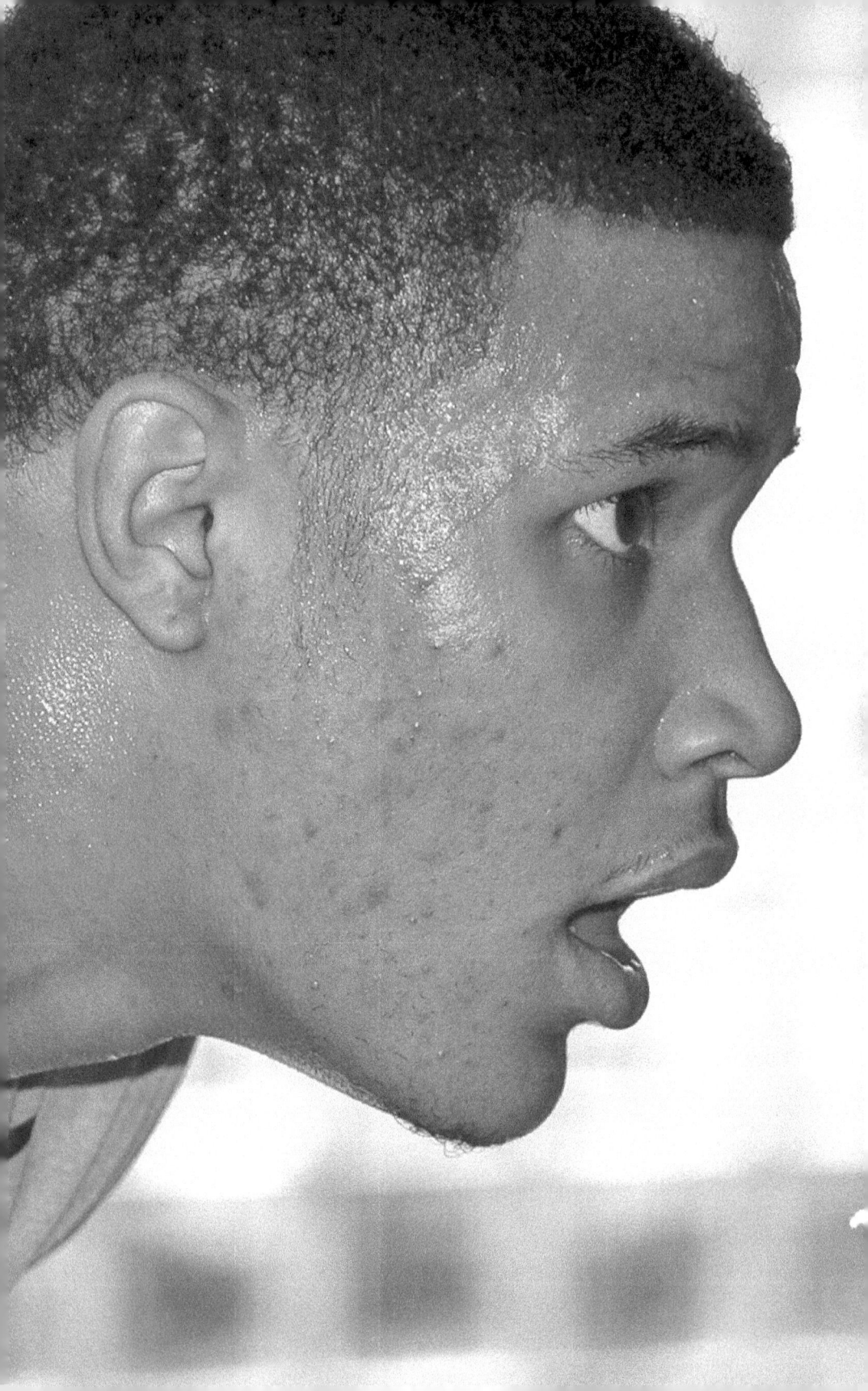

22. THEY CAN'T JUDGE WHAT THEY CAN'T SEE

Affirmation | Support | Blocking Out the Noise

When I coached at Iowa State, we finished last in the league. Because of that, we were picked to finish last or near last again when the experts made predictions for the upcoming season. They assumed, based on the team we were previously, that there was no chance there would be a championship in our future forecast. While those on the outside predicted we would not amount to much, those inside the program knew we could have a championship season. Our unwavering belief that we'd have a championship year came from what we knew was happening daily inside our practice facility.

In addition to more than a handful of experienced players returning, we signed four talented freshmen. Two of them—Talen Horton-Tucker and Tyrese Haliburton—were underrated underdogs coming in. They developed in our practice facility much faster than anyone could have predicted. We also had a transfer, Marial Shayok, who sat out the previous year. Per the old NCAA rules, transfers could only participate in practices the first year and were not eligible to play in games. Mar, as we called him, had averaged just 5 points per game over three years at Virginia, his previous school. Of course, the so-called know-it-alls figured Mar would be lucky to average double figures. During the season he sat out, he dominated practice every day and was one of the hardest workers any of us had ever coached.

Aside from local media and a few friends of the program, our practice facility is closed to the public. So while the national experts were qualified to give their opinions on college basketball, their analysis of our team was incomplete because they didn't have access to the growth and development that occurred every day inside our facility. They didn't see Mar working out three times a day, adding more offensive skill and polish to his game, watching game film, and lifting weights every morning at 6:00. That's why they were surprised when he was a first team all-conference selection and is now a tenured professional player. They also did not see Tyrese showing the talent and point guard presence daily that would eventually allow him to be a first-round draft pick and sign a five-year, $260 million contract. Nor did they see that Talen was a man-child with combined skill and explosiveness that would propel him to become a one-and-done NBA talent and NBA champion.

The internal development behind closed doors produced an expectancy of success for the team, despite what the so-called experts thought. That fueled the team, the one everyone had dismissed to go on and win the Big 12 championship. I don't believe our team would have come close to winning a championship had they allowed themselves to be impacted by the opinions of those without access to the inside.

The same goes for all of us. If we let the opinions of those who cannot see what's being developed within us discourage us from believing we are champions destined for winning moments, we are far less likely to reach our potential.

OVERTIME

Never allow someone who doesn't have access to the inside project what you can achieve. Learn from that Iowa State team that it matters not if those on the outside are experts who appear to know it all. If they do not have access to what's being developed on the inside, then their opinions are inaccurate and must be disqualified.

What's being developed within you, much like that championship team, will eventually show up for the outside world to see. That will happen as long as you keep doing the work and remain unbothered by the opinions, the energy, and the projections of those on the outside—expert or not!

Who an underdog was has no influence on who that underdog will become—as long as they commit to continual internal development.

LEMON DROPS

"Work in silence and let 'em sleep on you. The noise from your success will wake 'em up in due time."
— TONY GASKINS

"A seed grows with no sound, but a tree falls with a huge noise. Destruction has noise, but creation is quiet. This is the power of silence. Grow silently."
— CONFUCIUS

"Accept and acknowledge your own brilliance. Stop waiting for others to tell you how great you are! Believe it for yourself and about yourself."
— IYANLA VANZANT

"Whenever you see a successful person, you only see the public glories, never the private sacrifices to reach them."
— VAIBHAV SHAH

23. BRITTANY GRAHAM: SOMETIMES IMPATIENCE IS LEGITIMIZED

Encouragement | Hope | Nourishment | Reparation
Understanding | Mental Health

In Martin Luther King Jr.'s. "Letter from Birmingham Jail," he wrote, "I hope, sirs, that you can understand our legitimate and unavoidable impatience." Life is about balance. There are circumstances in life when you must be patient, allow your deep roots to fully develop, and wait for your opportunity. But there are other times when you must realize your roots are deep and developed and that it's time to relinquish your patient temperament and go take the opportunity that's rightfully yours.

To give context to MLK's reference to legitimate impatience, he was writing from jail during the Civil Rights Movement. He wrote, "Oppressed people cannot remain oppressed forever. The urge for freedom will eventually come. This is what has happened to the American Negro. Something within has reminded him of his birthright of freedom; something without has reminded him that he can gain it."

Long before MLK, a second-generation slave, Robert Smalls, navigated himself and 17 others out of slavery. Smalls not only became free but became a Navy captain and a state senator. While enslaved, Smalls was allowed to keep $1 each time he was "paid" for his work. After he saved $100, he inquired about purchasing his family from the slave owner. They agreed but said the price was $800!

Instead of remaining patient, in 1862, Smalls overtook the gunboat CSS *Planter* through determination, preparation, fearlessness, and intelligence, and sailed to freedom. What Smalls did was so impressive that he not only was free but was recognized for his courage and intelligence The U.S. Congress awarded Smalls and his crew prize money (Small's share was $1,500) for returning the *Planter*. Smalls eventually became captain of the *Planter* and then a state senator. His legitimized impatience empowered him to go from a slave to a place of political power. Had he chosen patience, there's a chance he would never have been able to buy his freedom or become a captain and a senator who could impact those around him for the better.

People like MLK and Smalls are my heroes, but one of my current-day heroes is my sister, Brittany. She is the most creative person I know and embodies the same legitimized impatient energy that King spoke of and Smalls lived. Along with being the best shooter in the family, Brittany is a self-taught, self-made sports photographer. She's a basketball streetwear designer and an athletic content creator extraordinaire for high school basketball national champion Duncanville (Texas) High School.

Brittany loves major college sports—college football in particular. Her dream was to be on staff for a team at a power conference with a top-tier football team. Because of her creativity, talent, work ethic, and personality, she landed what appeared to be a dream job as the content creator for the basketball team at one of the biggest college athletic brands in the country. We'll call the school Cap State. To make it even sweeter, their football team was one of the powers of college football. One of her many perks included two season tickets to the football games.

Unfortunately, the job was not what it appeared to be. Frederick Haynes III warns that those with a spirit of excellence, like Brittany, must be on the lookout for mediocre supervisors because professionally speaking, "Whenever you aspire for excellence, those that are mediocre see you as the enemy. As you live your best life, while they choose to live their worst life and can't handle your best life, they will somehow make you their enemy."

BRITTANY GRAHAM: SOMETIMES IMPATIENCE IS LEGITIMIZED

That was the case with Brittany. Her supervisor, we'll call her Coach Cap, micromanaged her in order to minimize her talent. Brittany's creativity was frowned upon and at times outright forbidden. Every time she ventured outside the tiny creative box she was far too talented to dwell in, they reprimanded her and implored her to "stay patient." On occasion, they even threatened her job. Crazy, right? Imagine being hired for your creativity only to be reprimanded for being creative. If that wasn't difficult enough, the job was half across the country, which meant she was far removed from all her root encouraging family and friends. Aside from her wonder dog, my fur-niece Harper, Brittany had to endure her battle alone.

That placed Brittany at an underdog crossroads. She could choose to play it safe, make decent money, settle for a fraction of her professional desires, and "be patient." Suppose she chose to go in that direction. Possibly in a few years they'd give her a longer creative leash in exchange for her agreeing to live in the small, uncreative box that had allowed her to keep her job but would leave her unfulfilled and professionally depressed. Instead of playing safe and compromising her creative gifts, she chose to courageously and impatiently be "dareful" and walk away from what she once assumed was her dream job.

In the spirit of MLK, Brittany committed to risking it all in order to be treated the way she deserved! Her next move was to Dallas where she'd eventually launch her own brand—Foreverland. But before she was able to do that, she had to heal from the deep, dark professional depression that Coach Cap at Cap State had caused.

Brittany was so despondent that she didn't leave her bedroom for three weeks. Her confidence was so broken that she was too fragile to do what she loved. At the time, I was helping NBA basketball player Buddy Hield and his trainer prepare for the upcoming season. I invited Brittany to the workout to take photos. She once would have jumped at that opportunity, but because of Coach Cap and her professional heartbreak, she didn't have it in her.

A few weeks passed, and Brittany, with the support of her root encouragers, developed enough mental strength and did enough healing to bravely go to Buddy's workout. Of course, being the GOAT (Greatest of All Time) that she is, Buddy loved her work and immediately posted her photos on his IG. His team at the time, the Sacramento Kings, also reposted her images. Shortly after that, many of the top NBA and college players, along with high school teams in Texas, began hiring her to shoot their workouts, practices, and games.

Before long, Brittany went from being treated like a nobody to more than just a somebody. She's now local basketball royalty, part of the basketball culture and a role model and inspiration to young women throughout competitive athletics. Her brand, Foreverland, is worn by all the top high schools and endorsed by the top players in Texas. She has her own national basketball tournament, and most importantly, when she arrived at her underdog crossroads, she correctly and tenaciously chose to live her best life and not be content with a settled life.

As we underdogs look to pursue excellence and reach our potential, we establish our underdog DNA and honor the underdog code. We must not be caught off guard if those in power—a coach, a family member, a supervisor, or someone else—overlook, dismiss, discount, and maybe even disrespect us.

If that ever happens, we must recognize that they may gaslight us by insisting that we just remain patient and know that our time is coming. What we have to know is that it could be time to legitimize our impatience and, much like Brittany, never settle. It could be time to take over through our dedication, preparation, fearlessness, and intelligence, just like Captain Smalls.

OVERTIME

Recently, Brittany was offered a job in the same conference as the school she worked at previously. The job she was offered was much better than the one she had. While Brittany appreciated the consideration, she immediately turned the job down because the business she had built for herself was more lucrative, and more importantly, she was wholly fulfilled professionally.

BRITTANY GRAHAM: SOMETIMES IMPATIENCE IS LEGITIMIZED

When people motivate us to work so hard that we live out our dreams, our dreams become our reality. My hope for all underdogs is that, like Brittany, we will work so hard that our current reality is bigger than our biggest dreams!

LEMON DROPS

"Security is mostly a superstition. It does not exist in nature, nor do the children of men as a whole experience it."
— HELEN KELLER

"Avoiding danger is no safer in the long run than outright exposure. . . . Life is either a daring adventure or nothing."
— HELEN KELLER

"Only when we are no longer afraid do we begin to live."
— DOROTHY THOMPSON

"Don't be afraid to go out on a limb. That's where the fruit is."
— H. JACKSON BROWNE

"Keep some room in your heart for the unimaginable."
— MARY OLIVER

24. ENDURE THE NOS – 1ST HALF

Understanding | Support | Resilience

At the time of writing this, I am recovering from two of the most challenging, unfair, darkest, damaging, and frequent nos I've ever experienced. Both nos came out of nowhere because the opportunities appeared to be promising. Before I tell you about the first no, allow me to provide context. I have been "professionally homeless"—moving from gym to gym—for a few years now. Because of my investment in my professional dreams, I am living on a friend's couch. My goal and vision are to contribute to basketball at a high level, whether as a coach or a trainer, while providing mentorship, fellowship, support, and holistic development for the athletes I work with, all while being able to earn enough to live life.

Over the years, there's been a lot of fruit as I have positively impacted many competitors. I was able to do that because I have never settled for being just an on-court coach. I've been committed to being much more—a character coach and a life coach. The fruit of that—lives that have been impacted—is far too important for me to settle for just being an on-court coach. That may be why some have been reluctant to hire me. Athletic directors and head coaches are focused on the coaching and recruiting demands of today's climate.

My dad coached in college for almost 30 years, and as a kid, I always dreamed of doing that, and I even prepared for it. I had come to accept that while I'd be good at it and it would be fulfilling, being a full-time college coach probably wouldn't happen for me. Then, out of nowhere, a Division 1 head coach called me as I was leaving church. Ironically, he had just left church as well. Despite only meeting this coach twice and never having more than a five-minute conversation, he asked if I'd be interested in joining his staff as an assistant coach. He went on to explain that he had been doing his homework on me, and that while praying at his church service, he felt moved to consider me for the position.

After a few days of meetings and discussions, he formally offered me the job. He told me to take a few days, think on it, and then let him know. What made it even sweeter was that he sought me out not just for my ability to coach but also for my passion for and success mentoring athletes. It was a dream come true! He said if I accepted, I'd need to be ready to move within the next week. After taking the time I needed, I decided to take the position. In the meantime, he told me to hit the ground running and start recruiting remotely because we had to sign eight players to scholarships (that's a lot).

Along with recruiting remotely, I began looking for a place to stay at my new destination. I started packing and setting up goodbye dinners with my people in Denver. After a few days, I had been on the phone recruiting for a few hours and then decided to take an Instagram break. The first post that popped up on my feed was from the university I was going to work for. It introduced their new assistant coach, the position I had been offered. The only problem was that the person they introduced wasn't me.

What appeared to be a revived dream and an answered prayer turned out to what felt like some sort of cruel prank and a gut punch to my soul that left me discouraged, depressed, and broken. At that moment, I considered walking away from basketball and coaching altogether. After a few days of crying, not moving from the couch, binge-watching *Suits* on Netflix, and eating junk food, I found the courage—with the help of my friends, my faith, and my therapist—to pick myself up and get back to it. I accepted an opportunity to train, mentor, and be the interim head coach of a 6A private high school in Denver. I had previously consulted for them. Unfortunately, this opportunity that I assumed would heal me turned out to also be a "no."

So far, I had committed to coach only in the interim. But at the suggestion of many respected coaches, I applied for the permanent position. While it wasn't a college job, it would have allowed me to fulfill my goals of coaching at a high level while mentoring as well. Because I had previously advised the team, I was included in the emails to parents. In the email, the school explained that they were committed to hiring a coach who would establish a culture of basketball excellence, holistically develop young men, and excel at individual basketball development.

Not only did my resume validate I was great at all of those, but after just a few weeks on the job, the players drastically improved individually, and we went 15–2 during the summer season against tough competition throughout the West Coast. All the guys had also developed a deep commitment to their character development off court. As the summer progressed, parents by the droves expressed their support and amazement at the team's on-court and off-court improvement. The athletic director assured me that if I wasn't chosen for the head coaching job, there would be a position created for me to do the two things I love the most—basketball development and life coaching athletes. That meant I would not be professionally homeless and no longer have to live on a friend's couch!

While I knew I was assured a job even if I didn't get the head coaching gig, there was no doubt in my mind (and in the minds of many coaches in the area) that I would be the next head coach. After our last game of the summer in Phoenix, I flew back to Denver. The athletic director had asked me to meet him for coffee. I assumed at our coffee meeting that I'd get the job offer or at least an informal interview for the head coaching position. The meeting started off great. He shared with me that he had never seen practices run as well as mine. He told me that he was in awe of my ability to lead and develop, and he mentioned how there was nothing but praise from the players' parents. He ended by sharing that I checked all his boxes and exceeded all expectations.

I'd like to consider myself a really good vibe reader. Based on this vibe, I just knew my job offer was coming. Unfortunately, my read was wrong. The conversation ended when he told me they were hiring another coach whose resume was comparable to mine. To make things worse, he told me there was no job for player development and life coaching. And if I wasn't down bad enough, he didn't even pay for my coffee!

HALFTIME

I vulnerably share my story of enduring tough nos not so you can feel sorry for me and not so I can vent or portray myself as a victim. I share this with you so you can feel my painful, heartbreaking, frustrating, and frightful emotions, hoping you will realize that all of us underdogs must endure the nos. To do so, we must be emotionally tough, resilient, prepared, and strong. While this was extremely painful, I want you to know that I have endured and overcome my nos, just as I know you will too!

LEMON DROPS

"Life is 10% what happens to you and 90% how you react to it."
— CHARLES R. SWINDOLL

"We all learn lessons in life. Some stick, some don't. I have always learned more from rejection and failure than from acceptance and success."
— HENRY ROLLINS

"I have learned not to allow rejection to move me."
— CICELY TYSON

"If you aren't mad about the rejection, you didn't invest enough into the process."
— DARNELL LAMONT WALKER

"Realize your true strength when people reject you. In actual fact, they do not reject you. They only show you your real strength."
— ERNEST AGYEMANG YEBOAH

25. ENDURE THE NOS — 2ND HALF

Encouragement | Revivement | Nourishment | Perspective
Endurance | Preparation

While the personal story of my most recent nos was painful, just as some of the nos you've encountered, we must accept that nos are normal. Unfortunately, they are part of every underdog's journey. NBA coach Monty Williams once told his team, "Everything you want was on the other side of hard." And for us underdogs, everything we want is on the other side of a lot of gut-wrenching, unfair, disheartening, and soul-crushing nos.

While the notion that what we want is on the other side of many nos is simple, it dang sure ain't easy. Let's pivot back to our go-to underdog mantra—Nelson Mandela's quote, "Difficulties break some men but make others." Most people are not built for the underdog grind. But what qualifies us to endure all the nos that break others is that our emotional toughness, resiliency, preparation, and strength are abnormal.

To be emotionally and mentally equipped, all underdogs must understand Daniel Coyle's windshield phenomenon. Coyle explains in his book *The Little Book of Talent* that "we each live with a 'windshield' of people in front of us." When your windshield is filled with the right people, you have the best chance to reach your goals. Coyle goes on to claim that when we intently and frequently stare at what we desire to become, eventually, we will become what we've been staring at.

To justify his claim, Coyle references Se-ri Pak. Before Pak, there were no South Korean female professional golfers. However, after Pak won two major LPGA tournaments, she became the windshield for thousands of young South Korean girls. The result was Christina Kim's LPGA success. Kim, also South Korean and six years younger than Pak, became the youngest golfer to reach $1 million in earnings. Kim's windshield was filled with images and visions of Pak's triumphs, which prompted her to convince herself, "If she can do it, why can't I?"

My dad was also my college coach, and as you might imagine, that experience placed a strain on our relationship that unfortunately still exists. Even so, he was my windshield for my underdog toughness and resilience when I was growing up.

When I was seven, our garage door broke, and Dad got out of the car to manually pull up the door so he could drive the car in. While he was doing that, two masked men held him at gunpoint. My mother, my sister, and I were in the car with the driver's door open. The men tried to run my dad's pockets and then demanded that he give them all his money and credit cards. My dad responded by telling them to F-off and that he wasn't "going to give them a damn thing." While a shotgun was in his back, he pivoted and elbowed one robber in the nose. It was the guy who had the gun in his back. Once Dad broke loose, he weaved between two cars as he yelled at my mom to honk the horn and for me to grab my sister out of her car seat and cover her up on the car floor. His response startled the robbers, and they ran off into the night.

While that instance showed my dad's physical toughness, it fails in comparison to the emotional toughness he relied on to endure his frequent, soul-crushing, unjust, and unfair professional nos. When his collegiate athletic career concluded, he dreamed of being a Division 1 head basketball coach. If he was committed to following his dream, which he was, his Mandela-influenced underdog energy would have to remain on 100 because that was a fight that many like him rarely won.

When my dad began coaching in 1974, Division 1 African-American head college basketball coaches were almost unheard of. Despite most of the players being black, you could count the number of black head coaches on one hand. Even assistant coaching jobs at that level were rare for coaches of color. Back then, the status quo was there was only one black coach per staff. In comparison, when I coached at Iowa State in 2017, our staff was comprised of four men of color.

After a remarkable run as a head high school coach at Kimball High School in Dallas in 1982, Dad secured one of the coveted assistant college coaching spots at SMU, also in Dallas. The team thrived, and he proved himself to be a capable coach and one of the best recruiters in the country. The team's success and his coaching reputation led experts to identify him as an assistant coach who was next in line for a head coaching opportunity.

Dad applied for his first head coaching job in 1986 at his alma mater, the University of North Texas. But they chose to go in another direction. While the no was disappointing, his hope and optimism were unaffected since this was the first job he had applied for. He knew he needed to learn from the experience. He assumed that even though he was told no, he'd soon get his yes because of his path as an assistant. Unfortunately, that was not the case.

For 17 years, my dad applied for close to 30 head coaching jobs, and he was told no each time. Of course, all the nos were disappointing and heartbreaking, but many were also unjust and unfair. Of the many nos my dad endured, three of them stand out the most.

The job at his alma mater, North Texas, opened up twice more. While Dad was speculated to be the favorite both times, he was overlooked. Of course, this was gut-wrenching since he had been an athlete there, graduated from there, and even met my mother there. To make it even worse, the last time he applied, the school chose one of his coworkers. Throughout the year, my dad had confided in that coworker, assuming they were friends. That turned out to be the intel the coworker used to help him land the job.

The second no was at Wichita State. My dad always interviewed well, and as usual, he wowed the interview committee. He was confident that he would finally get his yes. One of the committee members, who was one of the all-time great athletes there, was driving him back to the airport. He pulled the car over and began to weep. Then he shared that although my dad deserved the job, unfortunately the committee had concluded that they were not ready to hire an African American. The compassionate gentleman hugged my dad, and they cried together. The man apologized on behalf of the school and then dropped my dad off at the airport.

The third and most painful no was after Dad finished his interview with the University of South Alabama athletic director. He was on brand as he knocked the interview out of the park again—and he received his yes! The athletic director said that he needed to look no further since he had just found his next coach. My dad immediately called my mother and told her the life-changing news. I could only see my mom's reaction—smiling and crying—and I knew Dad had gotten his yes. The athletic director told my dad they were headed to the president's office to inform him of the news.

My dad waited outside the president's office. The door was cracked open just enough so he could overhear the conversation. When the athletic director told the president who the new coach would be, the president responded, "Graham? He's a black boy, isn't he? We can't do that here." The athletic director had to walk back his yes, and my dad was dealt the most unfair, unjust, undeserved, and disrespectful no I've ever been part of. He returned home, much like after the North Texas no and the Wichita State no, and our entire family cried. My dad, the toughest dude I knew, the guy who did not blink when he was held up at gunpoint by two robbers, angrily and dramatically cried the night away in my mother's lap.

My dad was my windshield phenomenon at that moment. I could relate to his underdog soul and spirit. Growing up, my underdog windshield was flooded with my dad aggressively, relentlessly, and enthusiastically going after his dream. And when he was told no—no matter how many tears he cried, no matter how much anger he felt or unfair it was—he responded the same way. He woke up the next day, still hurting and angry, and went to work with a spirit of excellence and expectancy that his opportunity would one day find him. During his 17-year stretch of nos, he never missed a day of work. He was always the first one in the office and passionately worked late into the night.

Just because you do not see your next opportunity does not mean it's not lurking around the corner. Often, opportunities are senseless and will surprise you and pop up out of nowhere. That was the case for my dad.

Years after his most heartbreaking no at South Alabama, he had an unexpected phone interview with the athletic director at Washington State. Unfortunately, he had just returned from the dentist, and his mouth was still numb from the novocaine, so he probably sounded drunk! Despite that, he still interviewed well and was flown to Phoenix for an in-person interview.

Later that evening, I answered a call on our home phone. As I answered it, I heard the garage door open and close, which meant my dad was back from the interview. Just as Dad walked in, Rick Dickson, then-athletic director at Washington State, asked if my dad was home. As I gave my dad the phone, I could feel that this call was different from all the others. I could feel it. This was the one! I don't know what Rick said, but after about 30 seconds, my dad dropped the phone and began to cry. The hug he gave me was the most intense and passionate hug I've ever had. After all those nos, he finally got his yes. At that moment, I felt what he felt and what every underdog needs to trust in wholeheartedly—you only need one yes. If it's important enough when you receive it, it will be worth all the nos endured along the way, no matter how painful they were.

I knew how my dad felt every time he got a no. I had felt it too. I had fought the same unjust battle, only 40 years later. I had stared at my dad the underdog for so many years that I became that same type of underdog. My soul would never break, no matter what. If my dad could endure, so could I. And since I can endure, so can you. Keep going!

OVERTIME

I share my dad's story for three reasons.

1. Despite our strained relationship, I am so damn proud and thankful for his emotional resilience and toughness, and I want him to know that.
2. It validates why emotional toughness and maturity are needed to healthily and successfully run our underdog race.
3. While nos are sometimes harsh, sometimes frequent, and sometimes unfair, they are normal and will always be part of your underdog story.

You must be over-the-top crazy, committed, relentless, and unwavering to overcome your nos and chase down your underdog dreams. Remind yourself that you aren't alone.

- Walt Disney was told no over 300 times before he received his yes for Mickey Mouse.
- The creator of KFC's original recipe was told no over 1,000 times before the yes.
- Dyson vacuums endured 5,127 nos before they received their yes.
- Sylvester Stallone was told no over 1,500 times before he received a yes for *Rocky*.
- While attempting to invent the light bulb, Edison overcame 1,000 nos before he got his yes.

LEMON DROPS

"Stare at who you want to become."
DANIEL COYLE

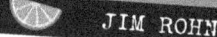 "Successful people do what unsuccessful people are not willing to do. Don't wish it were easier; wish you were better."
JIM ROHN

"Success is to be measured not so much by the position that one has reached in life as by the obstacles which he has overcome while trying to succeed."
BOOKER T. WASHINGTON

"Winning is great, sure, but if you are really going to do something in life, the secret is learning how to lose. Nobody goes undefeated all the time. If you can pick up after a crushing defeat, and go on to win again, you are going to be a champion someday."
WILMA RUDOLPH

"I saw no results, I still woke up and chased it."
DEION SANDERS JR.

26. BRYCE COOK: LIVE IN LION

Hope | Affirmation | Encouragement | Nourishment
Revivement | Inspiration

A Turkish proverb states, "A lion sleeps in the heart of every brave man." Can we say it's up to you to wake the lion up? In most cases, our exposure to those in our life who have already awakened their inner lion encourages, inspires, and convinces us that we, too, can wake up that lion within us. When we wake it up and decide to live in lion mode, we will destroy everything and anybody that stands in our way.

I have been blessed to have had multiple lions in my windshield. But the most inspirational lion in my life is also the inspiration for this underdog movement and book. I'll never forget the first time I saw Bryce Cook play in the summer of 2017. In the chapter "Sweet Fruits Need Deep Roots – 2nd Half," I discuss how you don't have to look the part to become the part. If I needed to prove to you that this notion is fact and not cap, I'd just tell you to google "Bryce Cook basketball." You'd find videos of him standing just 5'7" yet having the biggest presence on the court. His high school teammate Auston Crowley once shared after a game, "He's small, but his voice is so big, so he's one of the biggest leaders for us, so we feel like with him, anything is possible."

During that tournament in 2017, Bryce played in his hometown, the new Mecca of basketball, Dallas. It was one of the biggest tournaments in the country against the best players in the country at the famed Duncanville Fieldhouse. Many of the players on the floor that afternoon are now NBA stars. Even though Bryce was by far the shortest player on the court, he was still one of the most impressive players and had the biggest presence in the entire tournament. After the tournament, I immediately became a card-carrying member of the Bryce Cook fan club and planned to influence the coaches to recruit him when I arrived at my new job at Iowa State.

As I've frequently told Bryce, I'd pay good money to watch him play basketball because he's worth the price of admission. He is a pure point guard, a natural leader, fiery and tough, and makes everyone around him better and tougher. While all of that's quite impressive, that's not why he's the lion in my life that inspires me to always live in lion. The following fall, Bryce, a senior in high school at the time, had just committed to his hometown school, Southern Methodist University, and suddenly he had a stroke!

Just 18 at the time, Bryce was healthy, well-conditioned, and a chiseled athlete. He was the last person you'd think would have a stroke. It was later discovered that he had a heart murmur and a pea-sized hole in his chest. Bryce chose not to feel sorry for himself. Instead, after a successful surgery, he began working on his comeback. Shortly after his surgery, he shared, "A lot of people were telling me I wasn't going to play D1. They said I was too short and I wasn't good enough. I proved everybody wrong, and that's what I'm still doing to this day. I may come back from this normal, I may not, but at the end of the day, I'm just thankful to be alive."

While on his road to recovery, Bryce suffered another stroke that affected a nerve in his foot. Because of the severity of his health, SMU would not clear him to play, even though his personal doctor and others cleared him. Again, Bryce refused to make excuses for himself and instead continued on his road to recovery.

In the fall of 2019, it was approaching two years since Bryce's stroke. Bryce called me and asked if I would train him. Since my status as a card-carrying member of his fan club had not changed, I, of course, said yes. We got it in Monday through Friday, both on the court and at SandersFit.

Three memorable moments are worth mentioning from our first workout.

- Bryce's winning and positive spirit, despite the underdog hell he was living, was impressive, contagious, and inspiring. Of all the people there, he had been dealt the worst hand by far, yet his attitude was the most positive.

- Bryce was not the same Bryce. Pre-stroke, he was a twitchy, explosive athlete. Post-stroke, his elite athleticism was snatched away from him because of the nerve damage and time away. It was the first and only time I have ever felt sorry for an athlete I trained. I knew I'd have to scale it down, so we began with drills I'd normally do with a basketball beginner. Still, he struggled mightily. Seeing the anguish on his face was tough to witness as he did all he could to move the way he used to. It was just not happening.

- Midway through the first workout, I huddled him and the third crew member, Chozen, a hardworking, overlooked hooper himself, to keep them encouraged and focused. I passionately told them that we were all underdogs and that "the world doesn't want to see us win, but we will win anyhow." With every word, both my passion and tone grew. I concluded by saying that because we were underdogs and "life ain't fair, so we have to outwork everybody and squeeze every ounce of improvement and potential out of every rep." From that moment, they both made a vow that they'd subscribe to the underdog code.

With every passing day, we embraced being an underdog more and more. And with every day, their underdog essence motivated me to not only keep fighting myself but to also write a book—this book—to inspire our fellow underdogs everywhere.

Bryce has kept that same underdog energy throughout his journey. We tapped in with one another from time to time. And every time we did over the last three years, it's been the same. He still hadn't found a school that would give him a scholarship. Yet again and again, he refused to feel sorry for himself and continued on his road to recovery and redemption.

UNDERDOG

There have been so many times along my journey that I wanted to feel sorry for myself. There were so many times I wanted to quit because I didn't see the light at the end of the tunnel. Still, every time I considered it, I remembered Bryce and how he always lives in lion, and that made me keep going through my underdog hell just like him.

In the middle of writing this book, I knew I had to tell Bryce's story. I just didn't know how. During that time, I experienced a case of writer's block that lasted all day. Toward the end of that day, I was ready to throw in the towel and call it a day. As I did, I picked up my phone and began to scroll on IG. Then I saw Bryce's post of him wearing a Sam Houston State (a Division 1 school in Texas) jersey and announcing his commitment. As long as I live, I'll never forget that day—July 5, 2023, at 4:17 p.m., It was the moment Bryce finally navigated through his underdog hell to redeem his basketball career.

After crying, dancing, and yelling at the top of my lungs, I called Bryce to first congratulate him and then to thank him. Confused, Bryce asked why I was thanking him. I thanked him for curing me of writer's block and, more importantly, being an example of what it means to awaken your inner lion. I also thanked him for redeeming his pain and allowing his lemons of life to be squeezed into underdog lemonade that has quenched my soul and many others'.

For me personally, it helped me endure the no of getting ghosted after being offered a dream job, the no of being overlooked and misled for the high school coaching job, and every other no I'll have to overcome. I then asked Bryce how he was able to overcome and endure. He told me that when he wanted to quit, he just thought about his grandmother who has fought and overcome so many underdog battles. He said, "If she can fight, so can I."

Bryce's stroke happened in November 2017, and he was not able to redeem his career until July 5, 2023. That's five and a half years of nos that he endured. His story gives us confidence to live in lion!

OVERTIME

It's the lion within you that wills you past the nasty nos of life. Between my nos, my dad's nos, and now Bryce's nos that were either unjust or unfair, I hope you are now convinced and comforted knowing you aren't the only one who has had to or will have to encounter unfair or unjust nos. Since that's the case, while there is nothing wrong with acknowledging how unfair your nos are, there is a fine line between acknowledging your hurts and dwelling on them. Be sure to not dwell, and instead, focus on awakening the lion within you that will allow you to push past all your nos!

LEMON DROPS

"I love my rejection slips. They show me I try."
SYLVIA PLATH

"If you aren't getting rejected on a daily basis, your goals aren't ambitious enough."
CHRIS DIXON

"Successful people reject rejection."
JOHN C. MAXWELL

27. GET WINS OR DIE TRYIN': HOW TO ENDURE NOS

Preparation | Support | Encourement | Nourishment | Challenge

In my opinion, 50 Cent's debut album *Get Rich or Die Tryin'* was one of the best hip-hop albums of all time. Suppose there was a similar title for our underdog journey. It might be *Get Wins or Die Tryin'*!

Rita Mae Brown once said, "Insanity is doing the same thing over and over again but expecting different results." While it may not be the official definition, doing the same thing again and again while the result doesn't change will indeed make you feel insane and appear insane to those around you. That was the case for Michigan football coach Jim Harbaugh.

We've already seen that underdogs must be emotionally equipped to endure a high volume of nos en route to their victories. But we haven't yet explored how we must tolerate those nos. It matters not if you are a football fan or even if you are a diehard Ohio State fan, which by default prohibits you from being a Jim Harbaugh fan. As an underdog, you'd be best served to allow Coach Harbaugh's insane example of maintaining enthusiasm while enduring nos to serve as lemonade to quench the thirst of your underdog soul.

Harbaugh's approach to failing embodies the spirit of Winston Churchill's definition of success. Churchill said, "Success is the ability to go from one failure to another with no loss of enthusiasm." This quote serves as an emotional roadmap for us as we bravely overcome our unavoidable underdog seasons of falling short.

UNDERDOG

Heading into Michigan's 2021 football season, Harbaugh was projected to get fired. Many so-called experts agreed he should have already been fired after the 2020 season when they only won two games. The expectation at Michigan, one of college football's bluebloods, is to win Big Ten titles and beat Ohio State!

On July 15, 2021, when Harbaugh addressed the media in Indianapolis at the Big Ten media day, Michigan had not won a Big Ten title since 2004. It was currently on an eight-game losing streak to Ohio State and had only won two games in the previous season. Harbaugh had never won a Big Ten title or beat Michigan's most hated opponent. In spite of taking nothing but Ls from his rival and coming up short every year in the team's quest for a conference championship, Harbaugh was insanely enthusiastic despite his pay cut due to his team's lackluster performance.

As you can imagine, most of the questions from the media were whether or not he was going to be fired. They asked him about the Big Ten championship drought and the losing streak to Ohio State. Here was his response to questions about winning a title and beating Ohio State: "Well, I'm here before you, enthusiastic and excited as I ever am, always am, even more to have at it, to win the championship, to beat Ohio. . .That's what we want to do, and we're going to do it or die trying."

Harbaugh went on to say that the most challenging thing about making the underdog climb is the fact that until you reach the top of your underdog mountain, everyone around you will attempt to influence you to give up. "Everybody is going to try and discourage you. Tell you there's no need to try; you have no chance," he said. Before doubling down on being committed to enthusiastically reaching the goal, he closed with this: "No, we don't subscribe to that at all. We're going to try to get to the top. We're either going to get there or die trying."

At the time of writing this, Harbaugh has not only led Michigan to beat Ohio State in the last two seasons but also to win the last two Big Ten titles! Michigan's new wave of success allowed Harbaugh to secure a big bag, and he was awarded a lucrative $36 million contract. Success leaves clues, and Harbaugh gave us one. We must commit to being insanely enthusiastic while believing we will get underdog wins or die trying!

GET WINS OR DIE TRYIN': HOW TO ENDURE NOS

OVERTIME

Harbaugh inspired me to write this underdog commitment of competition:

> I will lose some, and I will win some, but my commitment to myself is this: I will always compete, I will always apply pressure, I will get lost in the process of competing and show up with my swag on 100 always. While I hate losing, I can live with myself if I lose the right way. However, if I fail because I didn't show up or didn't leave everything out there, I'll admit I didn't stay true to my underdog roots. I am competitively insane. I will keep going hard in the face of nos, failures, heartbreaks, and hate until the result changes. I will do that while remaining insanely enthusiastic . . . or die trying!

DOUBLE OVERTIME

When it comes to your underdog dreams, are you willing to die trying?

LEMON DROPS

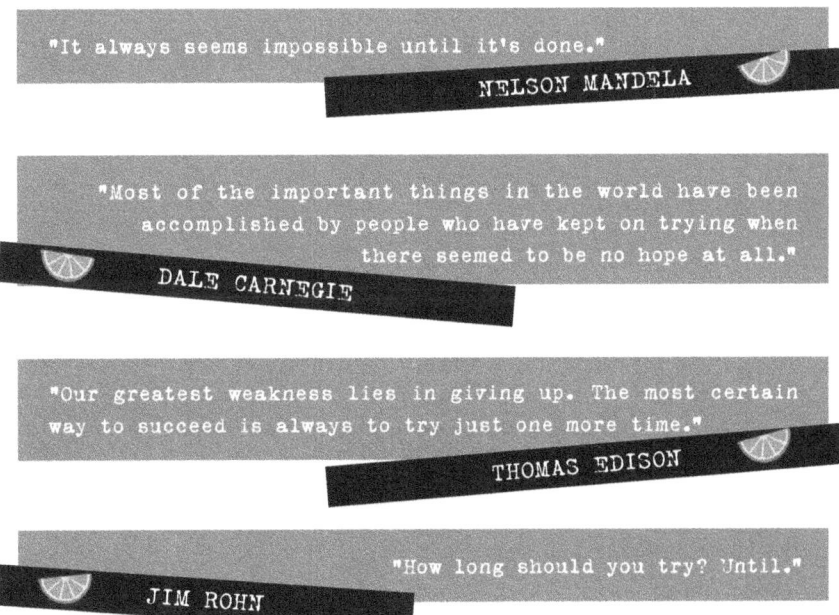

"It always seems impossible until it's done."
NELSON MANDELA

"Most of the important things in the world have been accomplished by people who have kept on trying when there seemed to be no hope at all."
DALE CARNEGIE

"Our greatest weakness lies in giving up. The most certain way to succeed is always to try just one more time."
THOMAS EDISON

"How long should you try? Until."
JIM ROHN

28. KARL PAYMAH: UNDERDOGS DON'T RUN AWAY FROM WALLS; THEY RUN THROUGH 'EM

Preparation | Challenge | Support | Spirit of Excellence
Perspective

One of my close friends, Karl Paymah ("KP"), an underdog himself, played in the NFL for six seasons. He once told me the story of the Grim Reaper. He explained that on every NFL team, there's a Grim Reaper. The Reaper's one and only job is to be the bearer of bad news and inform a player that he is cut. When the Reaper walks into the locker room, it gives funeral vibes. The music is muted, jokes and laughs halt, video games pause, and 53 brave gladiators suddenly become defenseless and crippled with fear. The Reaper, KP tells me, "always delivers the same message the same way. He comes up behind you and gives you a stiff tap on the shoulder, followed by the phrase, 'Coach would like to see you in his office; bring your playbook.'"

Unfortunately, when the Grim Reaper tells you to bring your playbook, you're about to get cut. "Guys tried to avoid the Reaper at all costs out of fear of being cut," KP explained. "They'd hide in the bathroom, the shower, their car, but it mattered not; the Reaper never fails to find his prey. And when he does, those of us who are spared, many after a change of drawers because they went to the bathroom on themselves, are just happy to see another day."

NFL contracts are not guaranteed, and most players are playing game to game, aware that their dream job can be snatched up at any moment. It matters not if a player has multiple years on his deal; the organization can cut him via the Reaper with no penalty, warning, or explanation. Even if the player had a great season the prior year, he could still get cut. A player could play great all season, have one bad game, and the following day, he could get an unexpected and unwelcomed stiff tap from the Reaper.

The average NFL career span is about three seasons. KP, being the underdog that he is, defied the odds and lasted six. My underdog curiosity led me to ask him what the source of his success was and what allowed him to avoid the Reaper for so long. He accredited his avoidance of the dreaded shoulder tap to his off-season preparation. He explained that he was not afraid to hit the wall as he prepared for the upcoming season. KP said, "I wasn't the best player on the team. At the NFL, everyone is really freaking good. So I knew I would not out-talent anyone, so my fear of the Grim Reaper led me to approach hitting the wall in my off-season training differently. Most others see the wall and avoid it. I made a commitment to myself that I would not run away from it, but by the end of the summer, I'd be able to run through it!"

For the sake of context, consider hitting the wall as your response to your challenges. KP went on to explain that guys preparing for the upcoming season fall into one of three categories.

CATEGORY 1: THE WALL (CHALLENGE) AVOIDERS

The majority of athletes are in this category. With intention, they avoid hitting walls in their workouts. They've mastered the exact pace to go and the precise effort to exert in order to get through the training while still having something left in the tank and never having an encounter with the wall.

CATEGORY 2: THE WALL (CHALLENGE) POSTPONERS

This group is where most of the rest reside. They go harder than the avoiders, but they try to pace themselves to make sure they have enough in the tank to at least make it to the end of the workout before hitting the wall. They prolong an encounter with the wall for as long as possible.

CATEGORY 3 (WHERE KP RESIDED): THE WALL (CHALLENGE) EMBRACERS

This group was the least crowded. KP says few are 'bout this life and suggests that this is where all underdogs must dwell. Like Morant said (the "Underdogs, Activate" chapter), this group wants all the smoke. While most avoid or postpone the wall, the Wall Embracers don't dodge, postpone, or run the other way. Instead, they go toward the wall with everything they have and hit it faster, harder, and more frequently than all the others. They are unafraid to empty their tanks during the workout; in fact, their tanks are often empty long before their workout ends.

Doug Wekenman once explained, "Cows and buffaloes can both smell storms coming. Cows respond to their sense that a storm is coming by running away from it. Buffaloes are built differently; they are set apart. When buffaloes smell storms, they charge into them head-on." It's much the same for people. While most approach the wall like cows, Wall Embracers relentlessly approach it like buffaloes. As KP mentioned, we underdogs know we won't out-talent everyone else, so we push ourselves to the wall and empty the tank daily to out-tough, out-care, out-grit, and out-grind our opponents.

KP says his workout did not begin until he hit the wall. That's when he found out what he was made of. He discovered how much pain he could endure before tapping out. He found out if he would break easily once he hit the wall or, if he was unbreakable, no matter what was thrown at him. By summer's end, he entered training camp knowing he was unbreakable because, as he said, "Early in the off-season, I'd hit the wall and fold, but every day it would be a little harder for me to hit the wall, and with every passing day, once I hit the wall I'd have more and more left in the tank to keep going. By the end of the summer, I was so prepared when I hit the wall, I'd run through it unbothered and unbreakable. That's when I knew nothing would break me, not even the dreaded Grim Reaper."

Underdog, as you prepare to advance past the adversity that stands between you and your destiny, approach it like many NFL players. Know that at any given moment, regardless of what you've previously accomplished, a Grim Reaper is waiting to provide you with a strong shoulder tap and inform you that your dream has been snatched. Since that's the case, you ought to—like our underdog inspiration KP— embrace and hit the walls like a buffalo, not a cow! When you do, you too will be unbothered and unbreakable. Keep going—through!

OVERTIME

When you aim to break the wall between you and your dream, avoiding it is not an option. Often the wall you could avoid is something you need to break through. Could it be that when you hit the wall it is nothing more than progress? Breaking through is painful, but with every hit, you're a step closer to your underdog destiny. With that said, how can you break something that you are avoiding?

LEMON DROPS

"It ain't about how hard ya hit. It's about how hard you can get hit and keep moving forward. How much you can take and keep moving forward."
ROCKY BALBOA, ROCKY

"Sometimes the only way to develop the substance needed to sustain long-term success is to endure a season of short-term suffering."
NICK GRAHAM

"The only way is through! Underdogs don't run away from the walls; they run through them!"
NICK GRAHAM

"Push yourself to failure, not away from it."
NICK GRAHAM

29. CARE HOW YOU COPE – 1ST HALF

Mental Health | Perspective | Reparation | Preparation
Prioritization

My most fulfilling course in graduate school was "At-Risk Youth and Coping." Before taking the class, I did not have a profound grasp of coping and how paramount it is to overcome the hardships we all endure. Coping is defined as how to deal with and attempt to overcome problems and difficulties. Youth (and all of us) need to be equipped with the necessary skills to cope healthily. In that course, we explored the importance of policies that implement proactive coping for at-risk youth, policies that provide them with the internal tools needed to endure and positively navigate through and healthily address the many problems and difficulties they cannot avoid. Doing so makes them more likely to overcome those hurdles and become prosperous, healthy adults.

In this book, we've talked a lot about relentlessly going after your dreams and squeezing every ounce of opportunity and potential out of your talent and ability. That's the standard and lifestyle of any committed underdog. If you've been on your underdog hustle long enough or if you've been reading this book, you know by now that you will frequently and unexpectedly encounter problems and difficulties while you're en route to your underdog desires.

Just like at-risk youth, every underdog needs to care how they cope. That will lead them to develop a game plan of healthy coping. Once they do, they can commit to sticking to it. Committing to a healthy coping strategy will increase their chances to prevail despite the underdog hell they've had to go through.

Unfortunately, most never considered or were prepared to cope before their underdog quest began. My hope for you is that after reading this, an alarm will sound as it relates to coping. The reason this is necessary is because there are two guarantees once you wholeheartedly commit to the underdog lifestyle.

> **Guarantee #1:** Life for an underdog is going to sho'nuff life (frequent difficult times will come).

> **Guarantee #2:** When those tough times come, you will cope.

While it's certain that you will cope, what's not certain is how you will cope. How you cope will determine if you are one of the chosen few who are made by the difficulties along your underdog experience—"Difficulties break some men but make others," Nelson Mandela. Consider what Virginia Satir, who's known as "the mother of family therapy," says. "Problems are not the problem; coping is the problem." My personal experiences validate Satir's notion. Coping unhealthily significantly decreased my chances of overcoming my problems. On the other hand, as I evolved into a mentally and emotionally healthier, tougher, and more experienced version of myself and began to care about how I coped, I was able to more healthily overcome my challenges.

HALFTIME

I've mentioned previously what Jim Rohn once said: "It's important to learn from your mistakes, but it is better to learn from other people's mistakes, and it is best to learn from other people's successes. It accelerates your own success." Remember George in Chapter 14? Once he established healthy competitive coping, he began to play burden-free, which led him to reach his competitive dream of becoming a professional basketball player.

While that was the case, he carried a heavy burden for the majority of the season. Had he established healthy coping earlier, his performance would have improved earlier.

CARE HOW YOU COPE – 1ST HALF

We can learn from George's mistake and his success. Prior to opening up to me, George, like many other competitors, swallowed his hurts and convinced himself he was being tough and that being honest with himself and others he trusts is complaining. Once George coped by allowing me to divide his hurts, he began to flourish.

LEMON DROPS

"I choose not to think of my life as surviving, but coping."
— LORNA LUFT

"You can't heal from what you won't deal with and ain't real about."
— FREDERICK HAYNES III

30. CARE HOW YOU COPE – 2ND HALF

Mental Health | Perspective | Support | Reparation
Preparation | Prioritization | Understanding | Empowerment

I want to share a few of my coping experiences with you, the unhealthy first followed by the healthy. But before we explore them, I want you to digest this thought. I believe it sums up why underdogs must cope. The thought is this: What happens to you can't defeat you unless it infects you.

COPING GONE BAD

After a year of coaching small college basketball, I walked away from it because I felt it diluted my life's purpose. As I mentioned in the chapter "Endure the Nos – 1st Half," I am convinced that one of my primary purposes is to use basketball to positively impact athletes and develop the character needed for those I mentor to thrive in life. With all the politics a college coach must navigate through, along with all they are required to do besides coaching, there was no way at that time in my life that I could coach at that level and stay faithful to my calling.

That led me to start Attitude 'N' Altitude, A N' A for short, which came from the mantra, "Your attitude determines your altitude." A N' A was a basketball and character development academy in Denver, Colorado. I built it out of the mud, brick by brick. I am not from Denver and had no ties to the area, which meant I was a no-name with no gym and no clients. So most in basketball circles looked at me as a nobody.

As you can imagine, I battled through many nos. But over time, I went from a no-name nobody with no gym and no clients to one of the most respected basketball trainers in Colorado and the entire region. More importantly, I was completely living in my purpose as thousands of young athletes were not only improving as hoopers but restoring their confidence, committing to hard work, and developing their character. I became so successful that when a national brand sports training and orthopedic corporation planted a flag in Denver, they asked me to merge my business with theirs. Since they had connections with NBA players nationwide, I accepted their offer since I assumed it would fulfill my purpose with a bigger platform. Unfortunately, it did not work out, and I was terminated from the business that meant so much to me and that I had built from the ground up.

At the time, not only did I not have any healthy coping strategies, but it was before I took the class on coping, so I did not even know what it was and why it was so important. As a result, how I managed with such a devastating and unexpected blow was not healthy, and I allowed what happened to me to infect me. I responded by working harder and angrier. I made no time to grieve as I convinced myself that those who acknowledge their grief are soft and non-competitive. Instead, I swallowed all that anger and poured it into my work.

I became a terrible friend and family member because I became possessed with proving that company wrong and did not deal with my hurt and anger. They say hurt people, hurt people. My experience proves that to be true. And not only do hurt people, hurt people, but the people they hurt are the ones closest to them. During that time, my sister made herself available to lend her time and talents to help me professionally. I frequently tell myself, if you don't face it, you can't fix it, and the anger and hurt I did not face led me to channel that anger in my sister's direction. Unfortunately, to this day, while my sister loves me, that dark period still lingers in our relationship.

Being driven by unfaced anger also blinded me from my purpose—why I was doing what I was doing. When I started A N'A, I told myself it was not about the money or proving someone wrong; it was only about the athletes I would impact. When I started, I never counted how many players I worked with that month or how much money I made until the month's end because I never wanted to distract myself from my *why*. What's crazy is that the more I leaned into that mentality, the more the money came in and the business grew.

While still in a space where I coped with my hurt by being anger-driven and committed to proving them wrong, I held a youth basketball camp. It was completely sold out, and in my mind, I had accomplished my goal of proving them wrong. My youth camps are usually the Super Bowl of basketball camps. The camps were a whole vibe, and the campers who attended felt the love I had for them (see Chapter 21, "Destination-Driven, Not Transportation-Focused").

I frequently run into camp attendees years after the fact, and they stop to share with me that my camp was the best camp they'd ever been to. Unfortunately, this camp was not like all my others, and the reason was because I was so blinded by anger that I had no love to give them and didn't know how to cope with my pain. And here's what was even worse. When the camp was over, I realized that those people from the corporate office, the ones I was living to prove wrong, could care less about me and what I was doing. And that angered me even more.

COPING GONE GOOD

Since my "coping gone bad" situation, I've learned that when we get cut from a team, fired from a job, replaced on a case, or overlooked for a promotion, it's commonplace to be encouraged by others, as well as being internally motivated and determined to prove 'em wrong. Perhaps we should pivot our perspective, and instead of proving the wrong people wrong, we ought to prove the right people right.

As I have developed healthy coping practices to deal with the many difficulties and problems any underdog faces, that perspective has allowed me to respond to disappointments from a much healthier place. Frederick Haynes III says caring friends "multiply your joys and divide your pains." When you prove those who couldn't care less about you wrong, guess what? They still don't care. On the other hand, when you prove those people right who have shown themselves to be the root encouragers on your team, not only are they there in the winner's circle ready to multiply your joys, but along the way, when life knocks you down, they will be there to divide up your hurts so you won't have to bear that pain by yourself.

In the "Endure the Nos – 1st Half" chapter, I mention the two painful nos I went through. Because of my now healthy coping, those nos that happened to me did not infect me. A significant part was proving Chris Dempsey, Chauncey Billups, and all my other root encouragers right. It allowed me to face and release the anger the old me swallowed and projected onto my sister.

Coping healthier did not happen for me overnight and is still a work in progress, but I would like to share with you the Mental Health/Coping Mental Hack I have developed for myslef: *Approach and view being mentally fatigued or sick the same way you do being physically fatigued or sick.*

While writing this, I had just gotten over a severe chest cold. Over the last couple of years, I have studied natural medicines. By doing so, I have become educated on how to significantly reduce the chances of becoming physically ill and, when I do become ill, what can be done to allow it to flow through as quickly as possible and in the least painful way.

So when I had a cold, I also had a game plan established for coping with it. After going to the doctor to get the diagnosis, I knew what foods to eat to reduce inflammation. I knew I needed to drink water and stay hydrated. I also had elderberry syrup to boost my immune system, Gordolobo tea to treat my bronchial cough, and my must-have, sea moss to run the mucus out of my body. Because everything I needed was already on deck, I was back to normal, and the discomfort and hurt had run through me instead of lingering around within, which could have turned into a severe and long-lasting infection.

The same holds true when I am physically fatigued. Being that I am a writer hoping to publish four books in the near future, a basketball trainer, and a mentor to many, it's incredibly taxing. That often leads to physical fatigue. To combat that, I have developed a diet that provides the energy and clarity needed to give me life when I hit the wall.

CARE HOW YOU COPE – 2ND HALF

It's much the same when I got ghosted after getting offered what appeared to be a dream job opportunity and when things didn't work out with private high school. I had the same approach. Because I knew beforehand that I would encounter difficulties along my underdog journey, I combined research along with learning from previous failed experiences to develop the following remedy of healthy coping that has allowed me to endure my nos.

- No more proving the wrong people wrong! From now on, prove the right people right and allow them to multiply my joys and divide my pains along the way. (That required me to be brave enough to tell them when I wasn't okay.)
- Be honest with myself about the grief and pain of the disappointment that allowed the heartbreak, anger, doubt, and everything else to flow through me and not linger and infect me, just as the severe cold did.
- Look at myself in the mirror to see where I can grow and get better. (I've discovered that when we feel we've been done wrong, we often become over-consumed by the wrongdoing that we fail to see where we can grow and be better in the future.)
- Meet with my therapist and allow her to coach me.
- Journal, allowing me to express my raw feelings healthily and safely, and work through them and release them.
- Minimize my social media intake and even hide some followers. I hide them not because they are doing anything wrong or even because I am mad or jealous. I have to be honest with myself and realize I am not in a place to see others in my field living the life that has been temporarily taken from me.
- Work out in group settings. Hard workouts with other "teammates" who love fitness have proved to be a healthy way to release my hurts.
- Don't avoid being alone when I need to, and frequently pray and meditate.
- Rely intensely on my faith.
- Watch comedies to force myself to laugh.
- Find healthy ways to keep myself busy, like writing this book!

OVERTIME

It was my pleasure to open up and be vulnerable. Now it's your turn! If you haven't already done this, start researching and developing your coping remedy to healthily endure your nos. Remember, be proactive not reactive. Find a therapist, start journaling, open up to your real friends, or do whatever else you discover that allows you to cope in a healthy manner. As you do, consider that unfortunately, somewhere there sits an underdog living with regret because they fell short of their underdog dreams. This underdog made all the sacrifices and put in all the work required, but they fell short because they did not care enough about how they would cope. Don't let that be you. Keep going!

LEMON DROPS

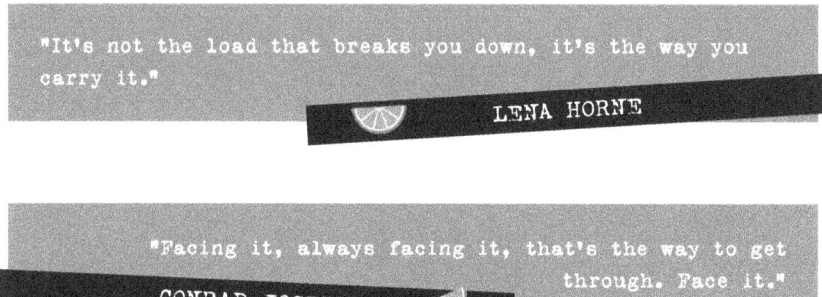

"It's not the load that breaks you down, it's the way you carry it."
— LENA HORNE

"Facing it, always facing it, that's the way to get through. Face it."
— CONRAD JOSEPH

31. MEET THE UNDERDOGS

Challenge | Perspective | Mentality | Spirit of Excellence

The Underdog family was set to move into a new neighborhood. Everyone in this charming neighborhood desired an elegant lawn with the greenest grass. In the community, the Standard family was the standard as it related to having the most excellent yard since their grass was the greenest anyone had ever seen. Each summer during the 4th of July kick-back, the neighborhood association held a lawn-of-the-year contest and awarded the prize to the house with the greenest grass. The winner received a trophy and a gift card, and was featured on the cover of the neighborhood's summer magazine. They also got a huge sign in their yard that read "Yard of the Year." As fireworks went off in the background, the Standard family, who had won the previous nine times, were announced the winner for the 10th consecutive year.

A few weeks after the event, the Underdog family moved in. Their house was directly across the street from the Standards. As they pulled in for the first time, they were in awe of the Standards' manicured green grass and hoped that one day they, too, would have extremely green grass. But they had a long road ahead. The family the Underdogs had purchased their house from had abandoned their yard care responsibilities once they sold the home, and the grass was dying. As a result, the Underdogs were the only house in the 'hood that did not have green grass.

During the Underdogs' first week in the house, neighbors came over to welcome them to the neighborhood. They were first greeted by the

Discourager family who brought over a home-cooked meal that included a famous homemade deep dish peach cobbler. As they sat out front and finished the cobbler, the Discouragers marveled at the Standards' green grass across the street. As they did, they began to compare the Standards' grass to theirs. The Discouragers, whose green grass was impressive in its own right, became so discouraged when comparing their grass to the Standards' that they lost hope, which is why they stopped taking care of their own grass. It gradually became less and less green, and eventually, it was not green at all.

A few days later, the Abandon family paid the Underdog family a visit. They lived on the same side of the street as the Underdogs. They did not cook much, so they picked up food from their favorite restaurant, Pappadeaux. It was a pleasant summer evening, so they all ate together outside on the patio. As they enjoyed the Cajun seafood, the Abandons, much like the Discouragers, began to gaze at the Standards' green grass with deep reverence. The Abandons inaccurately assumed that the reason the Standards' grass was greener was due to the side of the street they were on. The Abandons assumed if they just moved to the other side of the street, their grass would be greener and remain that way.

The Abandons, who had a history of abandoning their home in search of greener grass, had moved five times in the last three years. Each time, their grass gradually faded and eventually turned brown and died. Their desire to have greener grass prompted them to remain in a cycle where they abandoned their homes and yards and moved somewhere that might have greener grass. Despite the fatigue and frustration from all the frequent moving, the Abandons remained in this vicious and expensive cycle because their thirst for chasing greener grass was too important.

The last couple to greet the Underdogs, the Hater family, came over on a Tuesday, and it was only fitting that they welcomed the Underdogs with tacos. They Taco Tuesdayed it up! As the Haters focused on the Standards' grass, they concluded that it had to be artificial because there was no way anyone on the block could have greener grass than they did. It had to be fake. So the Haters were content with the greenness of their grass. Because of their contentment, while their grass had the potential to become even greener, it never got any greener.

MEET THE UNDERDOGS

After eating tacos with the Haters on Tuesday, the Underdogs spent all day Wednesday preparing a feast. The Underdogs had moved from Texas, the barbeque capital of the world, and Leslie Underdog, the mother, was a third-generation barbeque pit master. Assisted by her husband, Kennard, Leslie rolled out the smoker and prepared brisket, ribs, chicken, and all the fixings that go with it.

After preparing the mouthwatering barbeque, the Underdogs packed up the spread to take it across the street and share it with the Standards. The Standards welcomed the Underdogs into their home and were gracious hosts. It was a perfect summer night. The Standards suggested they dine outside on the patio as the sun began to set and an evening breeze settled in. Mr. Standard turned the Bluetooth speaker on and threw on his Summertime BBQ playlist to complete the summer night's vibe.

As they ate, drank, and were merry, Kennard Underdog complimented the Standards on their green grass. Kennard then humbled himself and shared, "Right now our grass is completely dead. Your grass is the greenest we have ever seen. We are inspired by the greenness of your grass and are blessed to be so close to such green grass. Our hope is to have the greenest grass we possibly can. Since you have the greenest grass we have ever seen, we were hoping you could share with us what you do to get it so green and help us make ours greener."

The Standards were more than willing to help. Still, they were surprised at the request since they had been living in the neighborhood for 10 years, and no other family had ever asked them how they were able to get their grass so green. The Standards explained in detail their recipe for green grass. The Underdogs pulled out their smartphones and took in-depth notes. As the night concluded, the Standards extended an invitation for the Underdogs to observe and even participate in their lawn care routine moving forward, which would empower them to apply what they learned to their own grass.

As the Underdogs applied the instruction they had been given and continued to observe and participate in the Standards' lawn care routine, their grass began to turn greener and greener. After a while, their grass was nearly as green as the Standards' and by far greener than all the other lawns in the neighborhood. Out of nowhere in early May, Adrianna Standard accepted a promotion that required the family to immediately relocate to Toronto. They were all moved out by the beginning of June, which meant there would be a new Yard-of-the-Year winner for the first time in 11 years.

With the title up for grabs, all the neighborhood families were reinvigorated with hope. All of them believed they had a shot at the coveted prize of having the greenest grass on the block. The Abandons, the Haters, the Discouragers, and all the other families frantically scrambled to find secret tricks and tips to put them over the top and ensure that their grass would be greener. They went on Instagram, YouTube, and anywhere else they could find to get a leg up. While everyone else was in a panic trying to figure out how to acquire the greenest grass, the Underdogs were cool and calm. They were empowered by the guidance the Standards had already provided.

During the 4th of July neighborhood celebration, as the fireworks went off, the Underdogs were announced as the winner of the Yard-of-the-Year contest. The Underdogs were lit, as they should have been, so much so that they decided to keep the party going at their house. They invited all their neighbors, and of course, they had award-winning Texas barbeque for everyone! While many of the neighbors were salty from taking an L, there was no way they were going to turn down the opportunity to eat some of Leslie Underdog's smoked barbeque.

This was a full-circle moment for the Underdogs. Last year, they had just moved in and had the only house on the block with dead grass. Now they were hosting the entire neighborhood on their green grass with the Yard-of- the-Year sign proudly displayed. As everyone dug into Leslie's tender fall-off-the-bone baby back ribs, Mr. Hater asked, "Leslie, how in the hell did you guys get your grass so green? Just last year, your lawn was an eyesore. It was the laughingstock of the neighborhood, and now you have the greenest grass around!"

As Leslie was getting ready to explain, everyone in attendance, including the Abandons and the Discouragers, leaned in to hear what she was going to say. Earl Discourager even turned off the music so he could clearly hear what their secret was. Leslie went on to say, "Well, like all of you, we desired to have green grass. Also, like you, we saw that the Standards set the standard for having green grass. The difference is, and I mean no disrespect, that we viewed being exposed to green grass with a much different perspective than the rest of you."

As many in the crowd began to give Leslie strong side-eyes, she dug deeper and told them, "In our old neighborhood, no one had green grass. While we desired green grass, we had no one to look to for guidance and inspiration, which resulted in never having green grass. When we moved across the street from the Standards, we felt it was an answered prayer because we now had someone to guide us to have green grass."

By now, the side eyes were turning into strong nods of agreement. Leslie continued. "When we gazed at the grass, we did not get discouraged and stop tending to our grass. We did not abandon our grass to chase greener grass, and we did not hate on the Standards for their green grass. Instead, we swallowed our pride, humbled ourselves, and asked the Standards for help and guidance."

Success leaves clues, and the Underdogs' uncommon perspective of being appreciative of being exposed to green grass was an example to the entire neighborhood of what can be accomplished when you move through life with underdog energy. It means you properly respond to being exposed to those around you with greener grass (more talent, experience, accomplishment) than yours.

That night the Underdogs stayed up with their neighbors until the sun came up. They were not partying but answering questions about how to develop and maintain greener grass while eating barbeque, of course. They even offered to host seminars, much like the Standards did for them, and every family in the neighborhood attended. After a while, everyone in the neighborhood was fulfilled entirely because their grass was as green as possible.

OVERTIME

Rick Warren once said, "Insecurity ruins relationships." That's often the root of why we ruin relationships with the talented people we are fortunate enough to be close to. Suppose we do not address our insecurities when we encounter gifted people. We will lose confidence in our ability and diminish our accomplishments, abandon our work and relocate, or outright hate on their accomplishments altogether. We've all been told not to believe that the grass is not greener on the other side. Well, sometimes it is, and if we allow one or all of those things to happen like the families in the story, that could be the sole reason we fall short.

Suppose we, like the Underdog family, check our insecurities, swallow our pride, and humble ourselves. We will begin to appreciate the talented people we are able to encounter and utilize them for the resource they should be along our climb. When we do, like the Underdog family, that may be the missing ingredient we need to reach our ultimate underdog success.

LEMON DROPS

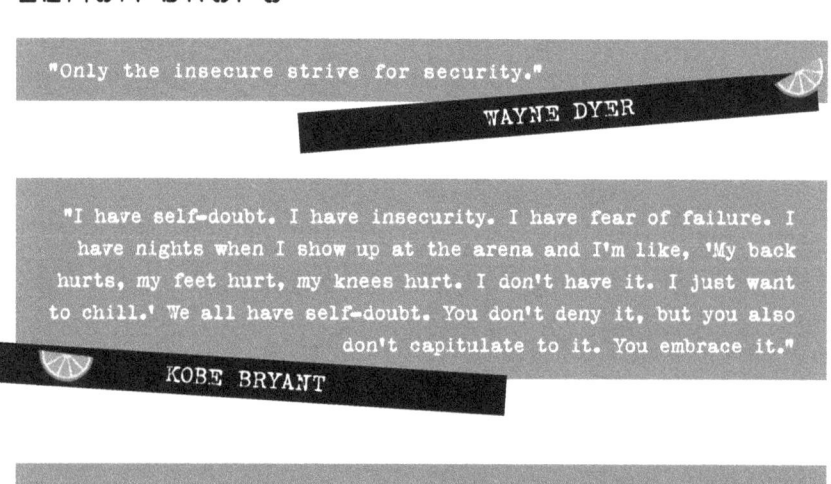

"Only the insecure strive for security."
WAYNE DYER

"I have self-doubt. I have insecurity. I have fear of failure. I have nights when I show up at the arena and I'm like, 'My back hurts, my feet hurt, my knees hurt. I don't have it. I just want to chill.' We all have self-doubt. You don't deny it, but you also don't capitulate to it. You embrace it."
KOBE BRYANT

"Comparison is the thief of joy."
THEODORE ROOSEVELT

Keep going

Even when it doesn't feel good

Even when it doesn't look good

Even when it ain't good

Even if when it's lonely

Even when it's dark

Even when you're hated on

Even when you're overlooked

Even when it's unfair

Even if the world around you turns its back on you

Even if they laugh at you

Even if you're going through hell

JUST.

KEEP.

GOING.

Don't worry about tomorrow; just keep going today.

Stay true to the promise you owe it to yourself to make and keep, which is,

ANY RACE I START, I FINISH,

which means,

NO MATTER WHAT, I WILL KEEP GOING.

Check out Nick Graham's first book:

GOD X BASKETBALL

Follow and Connect with Nick:

PERSPECTIVE COACHING - LEADERSHIP - SPEAKING
BASKETBALL TRAINING - INSPIRATION

ACKNOWLEDGMENTS

Thank you to all the underdogs in my life who courageously allowed the lemons life gave them to be squeezed into lemonade to be shared through this book.

Thank you to all of my "fog-lighted root encouraging" teammates who have invested in and contributed to me becoming the best version of me. There's no book without you.

Thank you to all the readers; I am honored that you have trusted me to serve as your "underdog whisperer" and coach you past your obstacles and push you toward your destiny. While I may not know you personally, I need you to know I believe in you. You are the "why" behind this Underdog movement, as I know one of my life's purposes is to ensure that underdogs never have to fight their battles alone. And through this book, you will never have to battle by yourself.

Lastly, thank you to the SOURCE of my Underdog strength and resiliency. I hope that You are pleased. I hope that I am hidden, and You are magnified. I hope anyone reading this book feels Your presence and is forever transformed.

www.ingramcontent.com/pod-product-compliance
Lightning Source LLC
Chambersburg PA
CBHW042138160426
43200CB00020B/2971